BIRD TALK

by

Caroline Dormon

Baton Rouge
CLAITOR'S PUBLISHING DIVISION
1969

Published and for sale by:
Claitor's Publishing Division
3165 S. Acadian at I-10, P.O. Box 239
Baton Rouge La. 70821

To all those fortunate ones who possess the magic "gift of the wild".

Courtesy The Sunday Magazine, The Shreveport Times

Over a period of years, these sketches appeared as monthly articles.

CONTENTS

ILLUSTRATIONS

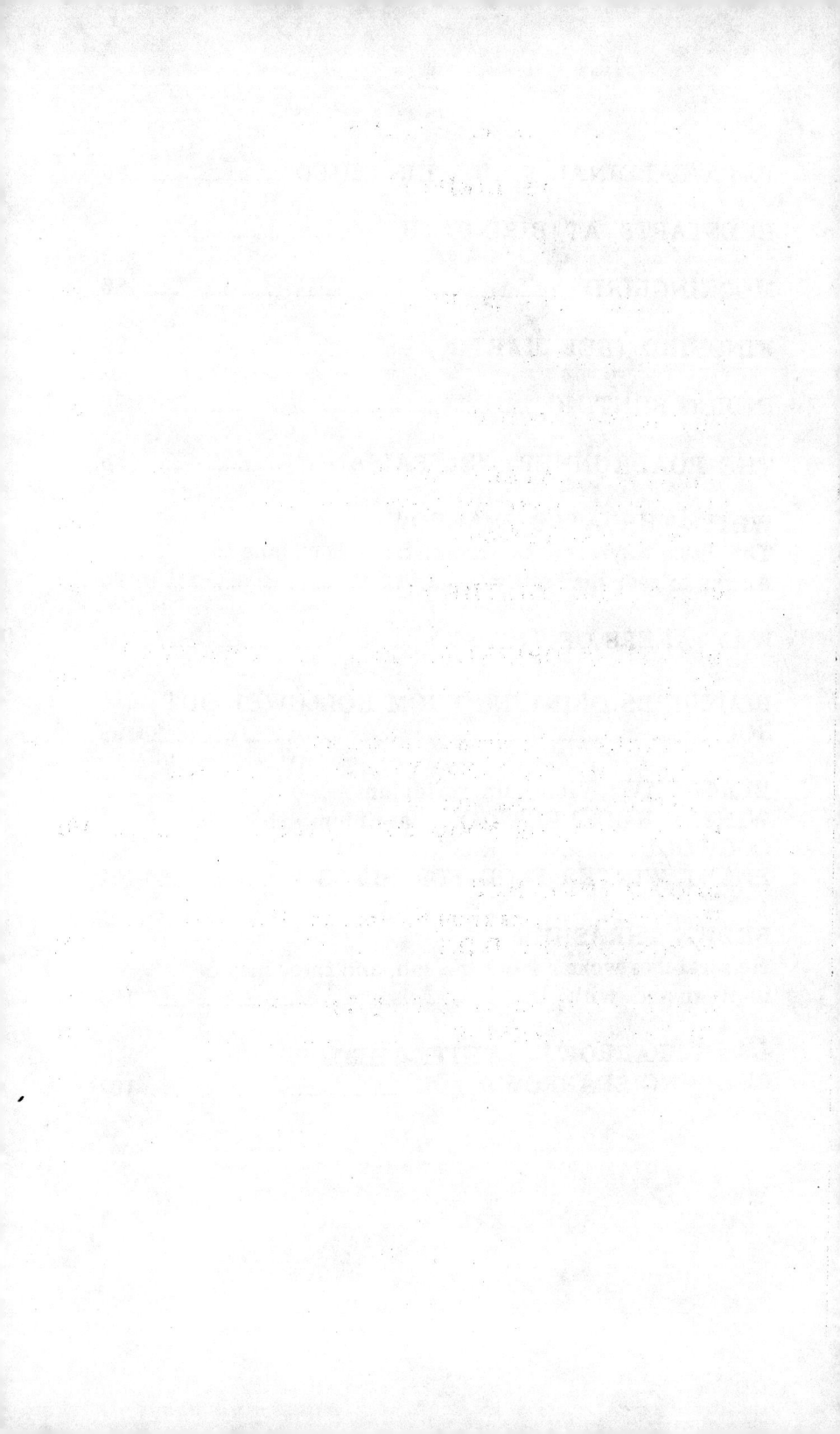

Bird Talk

LIVING WITH BIRDS

Around my old home at Arcadia, in the hills of North Louisiana, there were trees, shrubs and vines; so the bird life was varied and delightful. The term "bird-watcher" had not been invented then, but nevertheless I became one as soon as I could walk about the yard. From the first, birds fascinated me, and my father — a very good naturalist — taught me their common names. When we children did not know names we gave them those we thought fitting. One of the nicest of these was "Tot", for Kinglet.

In the next few years my older brothers and I roamed the nearby woods, climbing trees and crawling out on limbs to peer in birds' nests. We never touched them; just looked and marveled at the beauty of the eggs. Our father told us that if we touched a nest the mother bird would quit it! This was an exaggeration, of course, to implant the idea that birds' nests were "untouchables".

Through all the years I kept up my interest and study. Then when my sister and I came to live at Briarwood I at last had the perfect setting. It is in the sand hills, with small streams and mixed forests. The many species of trees and shrubs furnish a year-round food supply. In addition, I put up a number of feeding stations, which I fill with chops for the Finches and cornbread for insect-eaters.

In a retaining wall below my window there are big flat rocks with numerous crevices. In these I stuff cornbread, and Wrens, Titmice and Nuthatches assume various attitudes while digging it out. With my sketch-pad, I make "pencil snapshots". When wanted, I put these together and ink them in. Phoebe poses on a twig, waiting for me to toss her out a moth. Many species sit on light-wires, waiting for winged insects.

The bird-bath, too, attracts interesting models, sometimes rare and unusual species. Thus my sketchbook is filled.

1

There are some species, however, such as Great Horned
Owl and Roadrunner, of which I make composite drawings
from a number of photographs. The Roadrunner was the
worst — those legs just would not come right! I had seen
him, of course, but always in rapid motion. I *must* draw
him running. With pencil and paper I experimented long
before he moved!

Of course this book is not for the purpose of identifying birds — there are many excellent works on that
subject. These are just little chats, telling the things that
I have learned by living intimately with birds throughout a
long life.

THE BIRDS TO WATCH IN WINTER

Some persons think that when winter comes bird watching is over. They could not be more wrong, for when trees are bare we can see them better than ever. And some of our most fascinating species visit us in winter.

During the recent blizzard five beautiful Fox Sparrows came, so starved they tottered about as if drunk and had to SIT to eat. So seldom do we see this beautiful creature this far south that only bird-watchers know him. He is twice as big as our other Sparrows, with brilliant red-brown splashes on the sides of the breast — it is probable that he is often taken for a Thrush.

The Beautiful Fox Sparrow, A Rare Winter Visitor.

It is tragic that so few know that some of our finest songbirds are Sparrows. People allow boys to shoot "the old Sparrows" — lumping them in with that pest, the English Sparrow. The darling White-Throats come in October and stay till May, on warm sunny days giving us snatches of their lovely wistful song. The handsome White-

Crowned is a frequent winter visitor, especially in severe weather. What we call "Snowbirds" are the closely related Juncoes, in Quaker gray.

Another winter visitor from the far North is the Kinglet, that delightful midget. He can be recognized by his odd habit of constantly twitching his wings. He is soft gray, with a white bar across the wings and a red or yellow spot atop his head. But the latter is seen only when this little fellow is excited or angry.

Towhee (named for his call-note) is a year-round resident, but a denizen of bushy thickets, and seldom seen. In severe weather, however, he gets so hungry he comes to the feeding station. He is almost as large as his brilliant cousin, the Cardinal, but his pretty coat is black, white and bright brown.

A beautiful little bird is the Pine Warbler, olive green with bright yellow breast (the male). His habits are most peculiar. In winter he is quite friendly and eats at feeding stations, even when one is standing quite near. But let spring come and he takes to tall pines — even to nest — and we seldom see him. Occasionally we hear his high-pitched trill coming down from the treetops.

In winter the darlings of my heart are Carolina Wren, Chickadee and Titmouse. It is my firm belief that our Wren is the most cheerful creature on earth. Even when the ground is covered with snow he will perch on a twig and pour out one of his gay rollicking songs, which must give a lift to the saddest heart. He is never still an instant and how he manages to eat enough to feed this tremendous energy is a mystery.

Titmouse and Chickadee are closely related.— Chickadee with a black cap, Titmouse wearing a saucy topknot. These two and the Wrens are insectivorous species, and for them I cook cornbread — full of protein. Titmouse is more friendly (or braver?), and if one has the patience to stand immovable for several minutes he will take cornbread crumbs from one's hand. Chops are all right for Finches (Cardinals, Sparrows, etc.), so I mix some with the bread crumbs.

People often forget the birds have to drink in cold weather, as well as eat. But when once you see a poor little bird sliding his beak over the ice in the bird-bath you will be moved to pity and will pour water in it several times a day.

The only drawback to this whole program is that I cannot do any work for watching the birds! Just below my bedroom window is a low retaining wall, and there I spread feed. In digging out the crumbs, birds — especially Wrens — get into the most surprising positions. That is when I get my pencil "snapshots." Thus I console myself that I am accomplishing something!

PHOEBE AT DUSK
Waiting For A Moth To Be Tossed Out

In late evening Phoebe sits on a branch just outside my window, and when I toss out a moth to her she swoops in graceful curves and catches it. Then she comes back for more.

Gentle Phoebe spends the winter with us, and may be seen at dusk catching gnats and other tiny creatures on the wing. She is six or seven inches long, dark gray, with nearly white breast. She likes buildings, and will sleep on beams in an open porch. One has spent the winter with me for a number of years; and on cold rainy evenings, I love to see her perched on the edge of a basket or a rose vine safe under the porch roof.

Bird-watchers in winter can have delightful experiences and may record some rare visitors.

THE WAXWING, DAPPER DANDY

The Waxwing is the Beau Brummel of Bird-dom. His sleek, dashing appearance sets him apart from all other birds. His upper parts are soft fawn-brown, shading off to slate-gray on the tail, which is tipped with bright yellow. But the most unusual thing is the way in which his wing-feathers are tipped with what look to be drops of bright red sealing wax. His whole head seems to be swept up into a high crest and the eyes and chin are set off by distinctive black markings.

WAXWING
The Beau Brummel of Bird-dom.

Waxwings winter here in the South and travel in flocks. They seem to have had military training, for such precision in mass movement is almost unbelievable. Often they light in a tree and sit motionless for a while — with every bird facing in exactly the same direction. One expects to hear a command, "'bout face!" Suddenly they will take off, wheel in perfect formation, then settle back on the same perch.

They are said to eat insects, but here they feed largely on berries. They feast on berries of cedar (juniper), which has given them one of their common names, Cedar Waxwing. But they also love mistletoe and will crowd in to eat the white berries until the plant looks to be a bunch of birds instead of leaves and fruit.

But it is in late winter and early spring that we really get a close-up view of them. Then they sweep down to strip the hollies and privets. Sometimes they gorge themselves until they fall to the ground, apparently drunk. But George Lowery thinks that this is caused by the throat becoming so packed as to temporarily cut off blood to the brain, causing a blackout. Be that as it may, I have heard my father laughingly tell of Robins falling to the ground "drunk" from eating too many fermented chinaberries.

Waxwings' tactics in feeding are not always the same. I have a big holly which holds its berries very late, and not till the latter part of March do the harvesters arrive. The flock sits motionless in a high tree above and one bird at a time comes down to eat. When he has had his fill he goes back to the perch and another comes down to dinner. This may go on for hours, and in two days the tree is bare of fruit. Ornithologists have reported seeing Waxwings pass a cherry along from one to another, and claim this is because of their politeness and affectionate nature. It is also said they have been seen "billing" as Paraquets do, but this is probably during the mating season.

In spring these interesting birds leave us, most of them traveling as far as Canada to nest. However, they sometimes breed as far south as Virginia. We of the Deep South enjoy watching them in later winter and early spring.

GENTLE DOVE

Largely because of its habit of "billing and cooing", the Dove has become the widely accepted symbol of gentleness and peace. The closely related domestic Pigeons are often called Doves, but locally this term is reserved for the Mourning Dove. This name has been bestowed because to some persons their soft cooing has a sad sound. It is repeated constantly all during the nesting season. At this time couples often touch beaks in the most affectionate manner, and it seems to me that "Love Birds" would be an appropriate designation. They are often called Turtle Doves, though how they acquired this name I have never learned.

GENTLE DOVE

This is a rather large bird, about a foot long, with soft beautiful coloring, predominantly grayish-brown. In

the sunlight it shows a metallic sheen. There are a few
black spots and the side tail-feathers are tipped with
white. Feet and legs are rose red. It resembles the extinct
Passenger Pigeon, and the mistaken identity accounted for
reports that the former still existed.

Unfortunately, the flesh of the Dove is considered
tasty, and in season they are slaughtered by hunters. Their
swift and erratic flight saves many. In spite of the fact
that the clutch consists of only two eggs, their increase has
kept pace fairly well with the kill. This is because the
breeding season is long, and sometimes as many as four
broods are reared. Often they are still nesting in early
September, so it is a mistake for the open season on Doves
to begin in this month.

The feeding of the young is peculiar. The mother
regurgitates the food and the baby thrusts its beak into the
mother's throat to get a meal. The food of Doves is largely
vegetable, the seeds of all legumes being highly relished.
Sometimes farmers complain that their pea-patches are
being raided and use this as an excuse to load their guns.
But Doves are beneficial, as they feed on the seeds of nox-
ious weeds, also insects, especially grasshoppers. A favorite
food is the seed of homely goatweed, a species of croton.

It cannot be denied that the Dove is a slovenly home-
maker. The nest consists of a handful of twigs carelessly
thrown together in the fork of a tree. One wonders why
the two lovely white eggs do not spill out! The nest is
usually placed on a low branch of a tree, but once I found
one right on the ground. It was between rocks on top of a
high hill in the Kisatchie Wold in Natchitoches Parish,
Louisiana. At such an elevation I suppose the mother felt
safe.

SPRING RIVALS: MARTIN AND BLUEBIRD

Every spring there is a bitter struggle between Martin and Bluebird as to who shall occupy available nesting sites. Why don't people erect more houses for them? Martins come early and immediately begin circling about, looking for an apartment. Now, Bluebirds stay with us the year around and resent these newly arrived ones taking over their homes. Say they, if Martins are such softies they cannot endure our winters, then let them take the leftovers! Even if Martins have already settled in, the Bluebird watches till they are out, then takes possession.

SPRING RIVALS: MARTIN AND BLUEBIRD

Even the Indians loved Martins and hung gourds on poles to provide homes for them. This practice was taken up by early settlers, and poles hung with gourds may be seen today near houses in the country. Man-made apart-

ments are really better, however, with narrow porches
across the front for the short-legged Martins to sit on —
Martins are not perching birds. And they love companion-
ship, for few birds are so gregarious. It is my belief that
they like to sit on their galleries and gossip! I want Martins
for their beautiful flight, their sweet twittering and for
their throaty, gurgling laughter.

They migrate early, and in August gather by hundreds and sit on trees, telephone wires and crossbeams on
light poles. There they remain hour after hour, discussing
their coming trip. Some unfeeling persons say their twittering keeps them awake at night; they call the police and
have fire-hoses turned on the hapless birds! By late August
Martins are all gone south, and their going leaves a feeling
of sadness.

Folk beliefs are hard to shake off. How many times
have I heard, "I want Martins because they run off the
Hawks." Sheer nonsense! Our Martin is a Swallow, and
who ever heard of a Swallow fighting anything. Even the
gentle Bluebird can drive Martins away from nesting boxes.
The only plausible explanation for this myth is that people
have confused the Martin with the Kingbird (a Flycatcher),
whose common name is "Bee Martin." The latter is a valiant
fellow who will perch on a Hawk's back and peck him on
the head! But he does not nest in boxes, but builds his home
in the top of a tree. And he does not live on the wing, as do
Martins.

Our Bluebird is a close relative of the Robin, and both
belong to the Thrush family. If you do not believe this, take
a long look at a young Robin and you will see the telltale
spots and streaks on his breast. By the way, the American
Robin is not the Robin Redbreast of England, which is a
smaller bird. Early settlers saw a resemblance between
the two birds, so named ours Robin.

Another oft-heard remark is, "Oh, it must be spring,
for I saw a Bluebird!" In winter the Bluebird is shy and
seldom heard, so unobservant persons do not see him. But

he is here, and how it warms the heart to hear his soft
little warble on a sunny day! In severe winter weather this
little fellow probably suffers more than any of our birds.
His fare consists almost entirely of insects, and when
everything is encased in ice and snow he starves. But in
this desperate situation he sometimes eats certain berries.

One winter day, when everything was encased in
ice, I was tramping the woods putting out feed for birds.
At the edge of a field I spied a bush that looked as if full of
blue flowers. It was a sumac, with a dozen Bluebirds
feeding on the hard acid berries! Evidently these berries
supply some sustenance, for since then I have seen other
birds feeding on them. What makes the plight of the Bluebirds more pathetic is that they will not come to a feeding
station.

The natural nesting site of this lovable fellow is a hole
in a dead stump or tree, but he will accept man-made substitutes. A box should be about six by six by ten inches,
with the opening about two inches. It is advisable to put
the roof on hinges, so if invading English Sparrows take
over their nests can be cleaned out.

One often hears the expression, "Robin's egg blue."
Well, the eggs of the Bluebird are the same lovely shade.
Evrything about him is so attractive that he has come to
possess the imagination of a people and has become the
symbol of happiness.

He is not a denizen of the forest, but prefers the edge
of open fields. After a brood has been reared one can observe a whole family strung along on a telephone wire, right
by a highway. With the rapid spread of human occupancy
natural nesting sites are disappearing, so there has been a
nation-wide plea for more Bluebird houses. This plea is
getting a quick response, for few can resist the charms of
the gentle Bluebird.

THE SWIFT AND HIS COUSINS

To any but an ornithologist it seems impossible that brilliant little Hummingbirds and homely Swifts are closely related, but so they tell us. Swifts seem much closer to the Whippoorwills, for both have big mouths which they open as they fly, catching insects on the wing. They are small dark birds without a charm — except when in flight. They are really beautiful when they skim down the sky with grace unmatched, except by the Swallows.

HUMMINGBIRD   CHIMNEY SWIFT

14

Swifts literally live on the wing, never using their tiny feet for any purpose but to cling to the sides of a chimney. They even break dead twigs while in flight, which they fasten inside a chimney with their saliva. These glued-together twigs form a frail platform on which they lay their pure white eggs. These sometimes come to grief when a hard downpour runs down the chimney, softening the glue-like saliva. The nest falls, eggs and all. In Asia there is a species that fastens the nests to cliffs, and these are gathered by the natives for making soup!

The Hummingbird was the first helicopter. He can fly up, down and backward and can hang suspended in midair, motionless except for the rapidly vibrating wings. The wings move so fast that only a high-speed camera can "freeze" them in flight. He is so tiny that when he lights on a twig where one can really see him it is difficult to believe that he is actually a bird!

When Hummingbirds first return from migration they feed on a flower or two, then light to rest. Yes, they do migrate, flying across the Gulf of Mexico. This, in spite of the charming myth that they cross the water on backs of large birds. How can they store up enough energy in their tiny bodies to sustain them on such a flight?

There are more than a hundred species, mostly in South America. And there our own Ruby-throat goes to spend the winter. Some of the other species are much larger than ours and — unbelievably — a few are even smaller. Many are brilliantly colored, while some are rather modestly dressed.

This charming little creature has quite a temper and fights viciously. It is said that he aims his sharp beak at the eyes of his antagonist. When angry he utters a ridiculous little squeak which can be heard only a few feet away.

Tempted with the sweets he loves, the Hummingbird is easily "tamed." The late Mrs. Lillian Trichel wound soft bright-red yarn around a small test tube, then fastened this to a wire. When filled with water sweetened with honey or sugar it proved irresistible. At first she fastened the feeder to a nearby shrub where she could watch proceedings. But soon she could sit on an open porch and hold the wire while the Hummers fed from the tube.

There is no question that bright colors attract them. They hover constantly over Buckeye, Bottlebrush, Scarlet Gilia, etc., but of course they do visit other flowers.

The nest is a dainty little cup covered with lichen and set atop a limb. They are seldom seen because the nest is usually placed high up in a tree, invisible from the ground.

Summer would be incomplete, indeed, without these delightful miniatures.

THE BIRDS' IQ

People laugh when one talks about the facial expressions of birds, but their expressions are almost as characteristic as their coloring. Compare the bright inquisitive looks of Chickadees and Wrens with the placid gaze of the Thrushes. Thus birds display their intelligence or lack of it. The dull stare of a Robin suggests stupidity. (Of course I would be tarred-and-feathered for this in the North!) On the other hand, the lustrous, knowing eyes of Titmouse bespeak the wide-awake mind behind them.

The Titmouse proves his superior mind. When I put cornbread in a feeding tray, I call, "Come on, Titmouse, before the big birds get here!" I stand close by and the larger birds sit in the trees waiting, but one by one the Titmice slip in and snatch a piece of bread. This holds true of other little birds, too, such as Pine Warblers, Nuthatches and Chickadees. When it snows these small ones will eat from my hand.

There is an old expression, "He hasn't sense enough to come in out of the rain." Well, the Cardinal has. When my Lady Banksia rose ran over my front porch, some branches

ROBIN'S STARE IS EXPRESSIONLESS

17

extended under the roof. During a hard shower one or more
Cardinals would perch on these branches and sit it out. All
my life I have worried over the question of where birds
took cover during cold rains, sleet and snow. The smart
ones take advantage of the best places available. During
one protracted spell of snowy weather two Phoebes, two
Cardinals and two Wrens slept under my porch roof.

One of the most remarkable displays of intelligence is
the way in which some birds lead intruders away from
nests or young. Children — and most adults — chase after
a Quail fluttering just out of reach, to have the "crippled"
bird soar away when a safe distance from its babies.

Once the hired man said, "I've got a pretty to show
you!" I knew this meant a bird nest, so followed him to a
cotton patch. But before we reached the indicated spot, I
exclaimed, "Look, the bird is dead!" It was a lovely Kildee,
but lying on its back and twisted fantastically. When we
walked up to the "dead" bird it flew away! Then we found
the nest, a cup in the ground, holding the beautiful mottled
eggs. Some know-it-all scientists have tried to explain
away this wonderful display of intelligence, but their argu-
ments are too silly to even discuss. This canniness is not
possessed by all species. In fact, some birds scold and
scream at intruders in such a way as to tell the world just
where their nests are located.

The cunning displayed in concealing their nests is incredible. Vireos swing their dainty nests in a cluster of
leaves so cleverly that they are completely concealed. I
never find them till the leaves fall! Hummingbirds, Gnat-
catchers and Wood Pewees attach a little cup to the upper
side of a gnarled branch, then plaster it over with lichens
until it resembles a bump on the limb. By contrast, the poor
Wood Thrushes build their nests in the most exposed
places, although they are robbed repeatedly.

Call all these things "instinct" if you will. Let those
who may draw the line between instinct and intelligence.
I can't.

THE WEE ONES OF THE BIRD WORLD

The smallest of all feathered creatures, and the most amazing, is the Hummingbird. But he has left us now and gone to climes where there are always flowers from which to sip.

Undoubtedly the next in size is the Kinglet, a big-eyed, soft gray midget with two white wingbars. "But I don't see his red (or yellow) crown," you will say. Neither do I, unless I am in a position where I can look down on him. Even then I have seen it only a few times, for he shows it only when excited. It is strange that all the bird books,

NUTHATCH

KINGLET

CHICKADEE

PINE WARBLER

19

including the illustrators, give this as a mark of identification. A much surer way to recognize him is by the nervous twitching of his wings.

The golden-crowned Kinglet is much the same size and color, but lacks the white ring which gives the Ruby-crowned his big-eyed look. The former also has a distinct white line over the eye.

The Kinglet is such a little fellow he is afraid of every other bird. He feeds on tiny insects in trees and shrubs, but when winter weather is with us he comes down and eats cornbread crumbs on my rocks. When I see him on a bough above, I call, "Come on, Flitter-wing, while I keep the other birds away!" Then he lights at my feet and eats, while I stand guard — motionless, of course. Now I don't claim he understands what I say. I am just relating what happens. He is said to have a sweet song, but he saves it for his northern breeding ground. All that we hear is a whispered chattering.

The next bird in point of size is the Blue-gray Gnat-catcher, but he is a darling of summer woods. He is easy to identify, for he is a diminutive replica of the Mocking-bird. Winter brings back the dainty Pine Warbler. He is said to be a year-round resident, but I never see or hear him except in winter and early spring. He is a slender little fellow, with a bright-yellow breast (the male) and olive-gray back. He comes to the feeding stations for corn-bread crumbs and will even eat from my hand — if I am patient. The White-eyed Vireo stays with us in winter, but is inconspicuous and a little difficult to identify. His markings are very much the same as those of the Ruby-crowned Kinglet, but he is larger and does not twitch his wings.

The darling little Chickadee, with his winning ways, is loved by all. With his black cap and throat-patch he is unmistakable. It is strange, but he never eats from my hand, although he follows me wherever he hears my voice. I hear a soft little "cha-cha-cha," look up, and there he is on a twig right over my head, talking to me.

After the leaves fall is the time to see the little birds that find their food in the bark of trees. The tiny upside down Nuthatch is interesting to watch as he goes from top to bottom of a tree, feeding on minute insects and their eggs. The one most common here is the Brown-headed, modestly colored, but with a white breast, stubby tail and sharp bill that makes him easily recognized.

There are two other species with similar feeding habits, but they are a little larger and quite different in appearance. The Black-and-white Warbler "creeps". His clean-cut markings of black and white make him easily discernable. But Brown Creeper is so nearly the color of the tree-trunks he inhabits he is not observed until he moves. Up and down and around this little fellow searches the bark for insects and eggs. These small birds are invaluable to man, but are destroyed by injudicious spraying.

TOWHEE, PRETTY, BUT SHY

The Towhee, one of the prettiest of the Finches, seems to be little known. This is not because it is a rare species, but because it is shy and retiring. In winter if one hears a tremendous scratching and rattling in dead leaves it is probably the Towhee. He is looking for worms and weed seeds, as he eats both. The Brown Thrasher is the only other bird that throws the leaves about in such a manner. If the watcher be patient, he will presently see the bird make a short flight, displaying his attractive coloring.

The head, neck and most of the wings and tail are black, with white markings displayed in flight. The underpart of the breast is also white, but the sides are bright rufous-brown. This is the male. Where he is black the female is brown. The Towhee is almost as large as the Cardinal, but his beak is not as heavy and he has no topknot.

His name is derived from his bright questioning note, which has also been interpreted as "Chewink" and "Joree." In all, the first syllable is very lightly accented, the second sharp with an upward inflection. Like many birds, he is a

TOWHEE

22

ventriloquist and his call is difficult to locate. In his breeding-grounds he is said to take to the top of a tree and sing, "Drink your tee-e-e-." In the vicinity of Shreveport we are not treated to his bright little song, but George Lowery says the Towhee nests in the northeastern part of the state. The nest may be found on the ground or in a low bush.

Towhee never comes to feeding stations with the other Finches, but when the ground is covered with snow I spread food on my concrete front porch — almost flush with the ground — and he ventures to come there. This shy fellow demands plenty of places to conceal himself, so if you want his presence to brighten winter you must have some thick shrubbery.

It seems too bad that these charming creatures should be given such a prosaic name. However, it is appropriate, for their habit of catching insects on the wing makes them conspicuous. In other ways they vary very much, in size as well as in habits.

The gentle Wood Pewee is a sparrow-sized bird, soft gray, with head, tail and wings much darker. It will sit on a branch or wire for an hour at a time, occasionally darting upward to catch its prey, always returning to the same perch. Its plaintive note sounds as if it is saying, "Ple-e-ease!" in pleading tones. Its lichen-covered nest is set on top of a limb and from the ground resembles a knot on the branch. The exquisite eggs are white, the shell so thin there is a soft tint from the yolk, and with a wreath of varicolored spots around the large end.

WOOD PEWEE
(a Flycatcher)

Acadian Flycatcher is a woodland species, a little smaller than the preceding. It is soft gray with a pale wash of yellow on the sides, two white wingbars, and a white eye-ring that gives it a big-eyed look. It is so shy and retiring it is seldom observed. In open woods its soft "peet", or a sharp "pit-ee" may be heard. Its nest is quite different from that of Wood Pewee, as it is swung between twigs in a low tree. It is thin and made of horsehair and fine grass roots. The two eggs are cream with brown spots.

Instead of being gentle, Kingbird is the bravest of all birds, recklessly attacking Hawks and Crows. I have seen one ride a Hawk's back, picking it viciously on the back of the head, the Hawk diving and swerving to shake him off. But it is unfair to call him "tyrant", for he attacks enemies only. It is much larger than the two preceding species, eight or nine inches long, dark gray with a conspicuous white breast and a white band across tip of tail. He has been accused of destroying bees, and given the name "Bee-martin". This is an absurd charge, as ornithologists have proven that very few bees have been found in their stomachs. Books picture them as building nests on top of fence posts, but here they nest in the tops of rather tall trees. Farmers should welcome these fearless birds.

Crested Flycatcher is the odd-ball of the family, nesting in a hollow tree, gourd or box, and always putting a piece of snake-skin in the nest. The white eggs are streaked and splashed with reddish-brown. He is about the size of a Kingbird, but his breast and belly are pale yellow, and wings and tail brownish. He is a late-comer in spring, but tells of his arrival with a loud, strident "Quit-quit-quit-quit"!

The beauty of the family is Scissor-tailed Flycatcher. This exquisite creature can be recognized instantly, for it is well over a foot long, with a tail that opens and shuts as it flies. It is pearly-gray, washed with rose on sides and inside wings. It was strictly a western bird, but is moving into northwestern Louisiana and nesting here. It seems to favor pecan groves for habitat.

Gentle Phoebe spends the winter with us and may be seen at dusk catching gnats and other tiny creatures on the wing. She is six or seven inches long, dark gray, with nearly white breast. She likes buildings and will sleep on beams in an open porch. One has spent the winter with me for a number of years, and on cold rainy evenings I love to see her perched on the edge of a basket or a rose vine safe under the porch roof.

Only recently I learned that beautiful little Vermilion Flycatcher is occasionally seen in Louisiana. It is a bird of the far Southwest, and why and how it gets here is something of a mystery. It stays near ponds or lakes, where insects are plentiful. It is about the size of Wood Pewee, dark above, with a brilliant red breast. It is seen here in winter only.

CRESTED FLYCATCHER

TANAGER, THE WASP-KILLER

Often I am asked, "What is the red bird that does not have a topknot?" This is the Summer Tanager. He is smaller than Cardinal, and does not have a black face or a crest. He is not to be confused with Scarlet Tanager, which is a more vivid red with black wings and tail. The latter is often seen here during migration in April and May, but goes farther north to nest.

Summer Tanager may be seen wherever there are trees. The rather shallow nest is placed on a horizontal

SUMMER TANAGER

limb twenty or thirty feet from the ground. Here at Briarwood Post Oak seems to be the preferred tree, though I
have seen one in a pine. His song may be heard all day
long in spring. It is composed of about three notes and is
remarkably like that of the Robin. His alarm note is an odd
"chit-r-r-r!", quite distinct.

The Tanager's fondness for insects sometimes takes
a surprising turn. One day my colored helper came in and
asked, "What is that bird that's out yonder eatin' wasps?"
I hurried out to see. Red wasps had taken possession of a
bird-box and there was Papa Tanager, killing and apparently devouring them!

Only close observers notice the female, for she is a
nondescript olive on the back, with a dull yellow breast.
And what's more, the last of August the male takes off his
bright suit and dons clothes to match those of his wife.
This does not happen all at once and sometimes Papa may
be seen with red pants and an olive shirt!

Tanagers dislike cold, so they leave us in September
to go farther south, not returning till April. When we hear
him we can be sure it is truly spring.

Among the delights of studying birds are the unusual
and remarkable things they do. Once the colored woman on
my place told me, "There's a bird down at the house that
comes on the gallery and sits and sings right amongst the
children." Well! This I had to see, so down I went. Little
children were playing noisily on the porch. In a few minutes
in flew Papa Tanager and perched on the handlebars of a
tricycle. There he sat and warbled his little lay with the
chatter and laughter of children all around him! It was
perfectly clear that he was enjoying himself. Had he lost
his mate and was lonely? No one will ever know.

Those who want pretty Summer Tanager must have
trees. Some fruit-bearing species, such as mulberry, wild
cherry and elder are irresistible attractions.

WOOD THRUSH: SUMMER CHORISTER

It is April, and at last I hear a Wood Thrush. The mornings have been cold and frosty and not to his liking. Only after days grow warm do we see him hopping about on the ground searching for worms — his motions very much like those of his close relative, the Robin.

There is so much confusion about the name, Thrush, that it may be well to say a word or two on the subject. For example, the Robin is a Thrush, while the Water-thrush is not. (The latter is one of the innumerable Warblers.) When a Robin is first feathered out he shows the spotted breast of the Thrush Family. The big Brown Thrasher is often called Thrush, and he is a cousin. However, except for his size, he more closely resembles another cousin, the tiny Wren.

When warm days come this dweller of the forest becomes quite friendly and sociable. Here at Briarwood fallen leaves and twigs remain on the ground throughout the year, and here he searches for his favorite food. He makes a short run, then thrusts his beak into the litter, usually coming up with an earthworm. After this is swallowed he looks about, then makes another run. At this time he is almost fearless. I have dropped a worm off the edge of the porch, then stood motionless while Mr. Thrush hopped up and seized it.

If there are plenty of trees and comparative quiet, they will build their nests near human habitations. Again the resemblance to the Robin appears, for they gather a mass of twigs, on this place a cup-shaped platform of mud, and last, the soft lining. The three or four eggs are deep greenish-blue, very beautiful. Most birds conceal their nests

29

WOOD THRUSH

cleverly, but the trusting Wood Thrush seems to have no
ideas on the subject, perching his home in a low tree in
full view. This offers an irresistible invitation to the pirate
Blue Jay, who devours the eggs. I have seen nest after nest
thus robbed, and often wonder how Wood Thrushes ever
manage to rear a brood.

During the high tide of summer the song of the Wood
Thrush becomes outstanding. Even when the full bird
chorus is at its best these silvery notes are unmistakable,
especially in early morning and late evening. There are
some variations in the song, but the usual pattern is a series
of four notes with a question mark at the end, followed by
four down the scale, as if in answer. Now this does not
quite follow the chromatic scale, for there are quarter tones.
(Try to whistle it!) One bird seems to ask the questions,
while another answers.

When a summer shower has just ended in late after-
noon and a number of voices join in the chorus, there is
beauty not of this earth. There is no jumble of sound, each
singer seeming to wait until another has completed his
line, but the whole woodland rings with the silvery notes.
With the golden evening light, the drip from beech leaves
the only other sound, it is an unforgettable experience.

With all his sweet singing, the Wood Thrush has a
harsh scolding note, which he repeats when angered or
alarmed. With plenty of trees, and fallen leaves allowed to
remain on the ground, you may tempt this gentle bird to
come and dwell with you.

In the fall Wood Thrush departs for South America
and the Hermit Thrush slips in to take his place. This
change is accomplished so smoothly, and the two birds are
so similar in appearance, that many persons never realize
the exchange has been made. The Hermit Thrush is the be-

loved singer of the North, but he gives us none of his sweet
notes.

THE VALUABLE VIREOS

Of all the busy little birds, none is more untiring than the Vireos in the search for small insects. Inconspicuous, they slip in and out and under leaves and are seen only by the very observant. Their coats of olive blend in with the foliage of trees. In their never-ending search for food there is no estimating their value to farmers and gardeners. Not only do they eat insects, but they strip eggs from the underside of leaves.

Vireos are not easily seen, but they surely can be heard, for in their favorite haunts they "talk" all day long. They can claim little fame as songsters, for their notes sound

RED-EYED VIREO.

YELLOW-THROATED VIREO.

He wears 'spectacles".
And so does white-eyed.

more like conversation. This is especially true of the red-eyed, for he repeats his phrases over and over until the repetition becomes monotonous. He seems to say: "Here I am! Don't you see me? Well, why don't you?" He is a streamlined little fellow, about six and one-half inches long — the largest of our Vireos. His color is mostly olive, but his prettily-striped head makes him easily recognized. There

33

are no wing-bars.

The White-eyed Vireo is more than an inch shorter than the preceding, rather dull colored, but with two white wing bars, and he wears "spectacles." Instead of just "talking," he sings a sprightly little warble. As children we thought he said, "Fish'll bite today-ee!"

The Yellow-throated Vireo is easily distinguished from the others by the fact that the throat and breast are yellow. The back is olive, there are two white wing bars, and he, too, has "spectacles." He is not often seen, for he is something of a treetop bird. His "talk" is similar to that of the Red-eyed, but is lower in pitch and not incessant.

The Warbling Vireo is the most difficult of all to see, for his coloring is inconspicuous, greenish-gray above, whitish beneath, and he is rather small. As if this were not enough, he spends most of his time in the tops of trees, even swinging his nest from a branch far above the ground. His song is a smooth little warble of seven or eight notes.

All Vireo nests are pretty creations of mosses, lichens, thin pieces of bark and soft grasses fastened to the supporting twigs with spiderwebs. This sounds insecure, but usually the nests hang on through wind and rain for two years. They are so cleverly concealed among leaves that one is seldom found until after trees are bare in fall. The pensile nest of the White-eyed Vireo is the longest, about five inches, and is placed in a bush. The Red-eyed also swings his nest from twigs, but it is shorter. The nests of both the Warbling and Yellow-throat are shorter and more compact, and are usually swung in trees some distance from the ground. All the Vireos have white eggs with dark brown and purple spots on the large end.

EGGS AS BEAUTIFUL AS FLOWERS

Look in birds' nests, and feel the assurance that there is a Supreme Planner behind all things. Call it instinct, inherited memory, or what you will, why does the Oriole always swing his dainty cradle from the tip of a bough, while the little Chickadee seeks a hole in a tree for his home? Chuck-will's-widow makes no nest, so the eggs are perfectly camouflaged by taking the colors of the ground on which they lie. And these things never vary.

I can't remember when I began climbing trees to learn the mysterious variations in colors and patterns of birds' eggs, but I well remember inching out on a mossy limb of an old sweetgum to look into my first Blue-gray Gnatcatcher's nest. (My guardian angel had little time for loafing!) The tiny cup was set atop the branch, was made of lichens and plant down, and the pea-sized eggs were pale blue, with a few tiny spots. Seen from the ground, the nest was a mossy bump on a limb. The Hummingbird's nest is almost identical, but a little smaller.

The shy Wood Peewee makes the same sort of nest, except that it is much flatter. The beauty of the eggs is al-

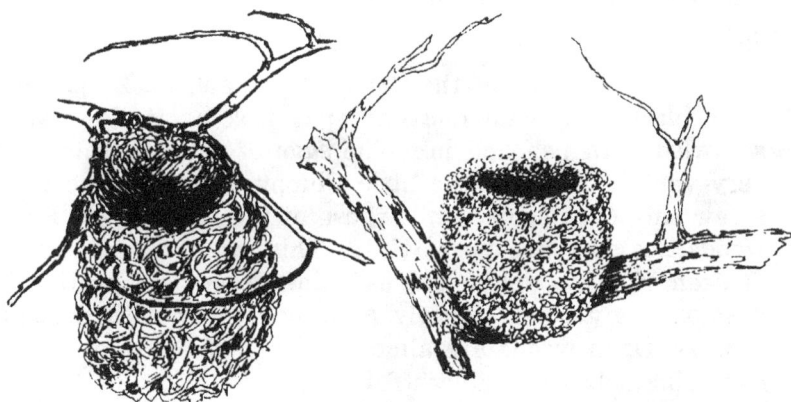

VIREO   **GNATCATCHER**

35

most unbelievable. They are white, but the shell is so thin
the color of the yolk shines through, giving them a pinkish
glow. Then there is a wreath around the larger end in
various shades of lavender and brown.

Quite different are the eggs of the Mockingbird and
Cardinal, for the colors are spotted and splashed all over
them. On those of the Crested Flycatcher the brown and
lavender seem to have run together, somewhat in streaks.
Those of the Brown Thrasher are so thickly speckled with
brown they possess little beauty, while the freckled eggs of
the little Wren are quite attractive.

Among the most beautiful of all are those with no
spots at all. The deep greenish-blue of the eggs of the Catbird and Wood Thrush is most unusual and lovely. The
Bluebird's are light blue, a soft tender color. Even pure
white eggs have their charm. As a child I found a quail's
nest with twenty, and as they lay in their grass-roofed
house, they presented a fascinating picture. I still remember how my heart beat with the excitement of discovery.
Eggs laid on the ground are pointed at one end so they
will not roll away — could this have happened by mere
chance?

The white eggs of the Oriole, Vireo and Lark Sparrow
have black marks on one end that look as if they were
scrawled with pen and ink. The eggs of the Sparrows are
very varied. Those of the little Chippy are light blue with
a few tiny dark spots, while those of the rather rare Pinewoods Sparrow are pure white. This sweet singer was a
denizen of open virgin longleaf pine groves and made his
nest on the ground, cleverly arching it over with delicate
grasses. Open woods are almost a thing of the past, so we
have almost lost this delightful fellow.

These are only a few of the lovely array to be seen
by those who possess patience and perseverance. Oh, one
who has never peered into a bird's nest has missed the
most delightful thrill of birding!

THE SPARROWS

The prevailing ignorance concerning our Sparrows is amazing. To the average person "Sparrow" means English Sparrow — that aggressive, untidy street-urchin, with its disagreeable chatter. Demonstrating the ignorance of our own charming species, these nuisances were brought over by two New England school teachers. They had the children sing songs of welcome to "the dear little birds"! Never had they observed the sweet songs and attractive ways of our own Sparrows.

When the boy with an air-rifle is asked, "You are not shooting birds, are you?" he invariably responds, "Nothin' but them old Sparrows" — and he has never been taught to distinguish between the unwanted foreigner and the delightful White-throat, which is about the same size. The latter comes to us in winter and stays till the very last of April. On warm days he treats us to samples of his sweet wistful little song. I have a friend who says, "I wish they would go on to their northern homes. They sound so sad they make me want to cry."

Not as common as the White-throat but often seen in winter is the White-crowned Sparrow. And when the ground is covered in snow and ice the handsome Fox Sparrow comes — sometimes almost starved. There is no mistaking this fellow, very large for a Sparrow and brilliantly streaked and spotted with reddish-brown and black. Song Sparrows are occasionally seen with White-throats. The two are quite similar, but the former shows dark streaks on its breast, with a black spot in the middle.

After the winter migrants leave we settle down contentedly with those that make their summer homes with us. The Chipping Sparrow is modestly colored and his only song is a high pitched little trill, but there is something endearing about him. He is a tiny slim fellow, softly brown-and-gray, with a white stripe over his eye, and the top of his head is a warm red-brown. Seven or eight come and

feed on grass seeds and bread crumbs on the flat rocks just
below my window. This is probably a family group from
the year before. In April they pair off and go in search of
nesting sites. They especially like small pines, where they
conceal the neat cup of fine grass-roots and hair. There are
four or five little blue eggs with tiny black spots on the
larger end.

In winter flocks of Field Sparrows are often seen with
the former species. These are just a little larger, without
the white eye-stripe and with a pink bill. The song is more
elaborate than that of the Chippy.

With the passing of hill farms one of our loveliest
Sparrows is going. The Lark Sparrow is unmistakable, for
his entire head is sharply patterned in broad stripes of white,
black and warm brown. He has another distinctive characteristic — he runs instead of hopping as do other Sparrows.
He is a ground bird, placing his cupped nest beneath a cotton stalk or low bush. The eggs are white with pen-and-ink
scrawls on the big end. He perches on top of a low bush to
pour out his lovely song, a sprightly medley of various
notes.

Another species that is vanishing is the Pinewoods
Sparrow. As his name indicates, he was formerly a denizen
of open virgin pine forests. He is a softly brown bird with
almost no distinguishing marks. His nest, on the ground, is
cleverly arched over with grasses and is almost impossible
to find. This is the only Sparrow that lays pure white eggs.
It is most easily recognized by its song — just a few simple
notes, but their purity and sweetness are equalled by those
of few other birds. Years ago I drove through a long leaf
pine forest just at dawn. I was in a buggy which made no
sound in the soft sand. The stillness was impressive. Then
suddenly the luminous air was filled with silvery sound, the
voices of the Pinewoods Sparrows coming from all
directions. The exquisite beauty of it still lives with me.

BEAUTIFUL ORIOLES

Lovers of sunny climes, Orioles are among the last migrants to return to us. When I hear the Orchard Oriole's happy, bubbling song I know spring is here. For a long time I don't see him, but his voice rings out from among the trees. His song is a varied warble, "When the green gets back in the tre--ees," ending on an upward note.

His nest is a pretty thing, usually constructed of just one kind of grass, skillfully woven. The stems are wound around the twigs from which it is suspended, making it quite secure. The nest swings, but is not a sack, as is that of his cousin, the Baltimore. Sometimes a few heads of grass hang down as if in decoration. The white eggs of both Orioles are curiously marked with black or dark brown

ORCHARD ORIOLE
(Adapted from a painting by Louis A. Fuertes)

"pen-scratches," and my brother used to claim he could read shorthand words on them!

After the eggs hatch the Orchard Oriole becomes very visible, busily searching flowering trees for insects to feed the babies. Mimosa and red buckeye offer a feast.

This Oriole is not so striking as his gaudy cousin, but his coat of black, white and ruddy brown is beautiful nevertheless. He is a slender bird, varying considerably as to size from six to seven-and-a-half inches long.

The brilliant Baltimore Oriole gets his name from the family colors of Lord Baltimore, orange-yellow and black. His head and the upper part of the back are black, and there are a few white splashes on wings and tail. All the rest is bright yellow. He is about an inch longer than the Orchard Oriole, and not so slender. His song is sweet, but not quite so varied as that of his cousin.

I do not get to enjoy this gorgeous fellow, for he does not like my sand hills and woods. This is a bird of orchards and open river banks. Down Cane River it seems to me that every tree is occupied. As the durable nests last several years, in winter bare trees look as if they have been decorated. These nests are works of art. The female searches till she finds some sort of strings, which she fastens to the tip of a bough, with the ends dangling. She then proceeds to weave in various other materials, finishing with a snug sack that hangs suspended about six inches. On the end of a branch, it swings with every breeze, but the eggs cannot spill out. Those who have these clever architects can help them by hanging pieces of string on bushes in nesting season.

Both Orioles seem to have a sense of homestead, for they come back to the same tree spring after spring. At my old home at Arcadia a pair of Baltimore Orioles came back to a big oak every year and swung their nest from the very same bough. And at L. T. Frey's home in Saline, Orchard Orioles have nested in a big red oak — the same branch —

for four years.

Just over in Texas there is a larger oriole, Bullock's, and just as brilliantly colored as the Baltimore. All the females of the family are more modestly dressed, with pale yellow breast and no black markings.

There are no more valuable birds than the Orioles, for their food consists almost entirely of insects, the hated boll weevil being a favored item. But even if they were not so useful they would be welcome for their beauty and their gay songs.

THE EXQUISITE WARBLERS

No other family of American birds is so numerous, varied and so beautifully colored as the Wood Warblers. Of the dozens of species found in the United States, George Lowery states that fourteen are residents of Louisiana. These also breed in adjacent states. The name "Warblers" is something of a misnomer, as only a few warble sweetly.

The largest of the family, and one of the prettiest, is Yellow-breasted Chat. As he perches on a bush his bright yellow throat and breast catch the eye. But does he warble? Oh, no! He utters a series of unmusical, ridiculous notes, with no connection whatever.

Maryland Yellow-throat is another species with a yellow breast, but it is much smaller. His unmistakable feature is a black mask over his eye and extending to his neck. Because of his insatiable curiosity it is easy to make the acquaintance of this dainty fellow. In the nesting season sit

MARYLAND
YELLOW-THROAT

down among bushes at the edge of a woodland, and if one has its nest anywhere nearby it will soon come around. It is a ventriloquist and its little "sic" is difficult to locate. But he will come nearer and nearer until within two or three feet of the observer.

Tiny Prothonotary Warbler is easily identified by his
brilliant yellow head and throat, but one need not seek him
except near lake or bayou. Instead of building a nest as do
his kinsmen, he locates a hollow, preferably in a stump
right over the water. Another peculiarity, he likes people
and will make his home inside a house! Because of his
friendly ways he was beloved of the Chitimacha Indians
of Southwest Louisiana, who said he spoke their language.
This required the poetic fancy of the Indian, for the
"words" of the little Prothonotary are not very varied!
Anyone so fortunate as to live on the shore of a lake can
put up a small nesting box and thus acquire this delightful
little creature for a neighbor. Male and female are identical,
which is most unusual in birddom.

Hooded Warbler is another striking species. The first
time I saw one, in the shadow of shrubs, I thought it was
a small dark-colored bird holding a little yellow butterfly
in its beak! Its face is bright yellow, surrounded by black.
Below the black, breast and abdomen are also yellow. There
is never any doubt as to the identification of this species.
And it is usually found near the ground in bushes and vines,
where it builds its nest. And it does warble a sweet little
refrain.

Black-and-white Warbler is so different from other
members of the family that it is often called "Black-and-
white Creeper," and creep it does. If it were not for its
sharply-defined black and white markings it would never
be observed as it moves up and down and around tree-trunks,
searching the bark for insects and eggs. It builds its nest
right on the ground, and had it not been for the keen eyes
of my friend Clarence Knotts, I probably would have never
seen one. He was walking through a forest when a tiny
bird fluttered out from underfoot, pretending to be crippled.
There was a dead pine stump from which a piece of bark
had fallen, forming a frail shelter. My friend looked beneath
this and there was the nest with five speckled eggs. He

called and asked the identity of the bird and then took me
to see the nest.

Pine Warbler is a modest little fellow, but a lovable
one. In winter he becomes very friendly and meets me at the
back door to eat cornbread crumbs from my hand. He comes
at my call. This continues into spring, when he will sit quite
near, lift his head and pour forth his sweet little trill. But
soon he takes to the tops of tall pines and I see him no more.
He is said to build his nest there, but I have never seen one.
This is a slim little fellow with olive-brown back and yellow
breast. The coloring of the female is much duller.

A queer Warbler is the Louisiana Water-thrush, so
called because of brown streaks on his breast similar to
those of Thrushes. He lives near tiny streamlets and hides
his nest in a hollow in the bank. As he searches for food in
the shallow water, he teeters as if it is difficult to keep his
balance! But now and then he perches on a low branch
and pours out his lovely sprightly song. It is as loud and
rollicking as that of Carolina Wren, but the notes are no
the same.

There seems little doubt that exquisite Redstart is conscious of his beauty, for he is constantly lifting his wings
and spreading his tail to display their bands of bright red.
In the female this color is replaced by yellow. I have never
seen these dainty motions exhibited by any other bird, and
they seem to express joyousness. Redstarts are denizens of
swamp woodlands, though they are sometimes found in dry
forests, but always near water.

There are other attractive and interesting species that
nest here in the South. And during migration season beautiful visitors may be identified. At this time I love to take a
bird book and seat myself among shrubbery. Sit still and
the hungry little things seem oblivious of the intrusion. In
a few minutes Myrtle, Bay-breasted, Magnolia, Chestnut-
sided and many others can be called by name. Alas, however,
a number of species are so much alike that it requires an

expert ornithologist to call the roll!

The value of the Warblers cannot be estimated, for in their ceaseless search for insects and eggs they are destroying the common enemy. What a pity that man cannot increase and employ this priceless host rather than using poisons to fight the insect hordes!

PREDATORS OF THE BIRD WORLD

The Southern Shrike fully deserves his common name, Butcher-bird. He seems to kill just for pleasure and hangs his victims on thorns and barb wire fences.

His defenders explain this by saying that he does not have strong feet like those of hawks, so impales small birds thus in order to be able to tear them apart. Maybe so. But why does he kill so many more than he can eat? I have found pitiful little Chipping Sparrows hanging by their heads, completely dried up.

The Shrike wears a handsome black and white suit, and is often confused with our beloved Mockingbird. But look more closely; the Shrike is heavy-set, almost "chunky," and he has a curved, cruel beak. Another common name, "French Mockingbird," is certainly inappropriate, for he is not French, nor is he related to the Mockingbird.

One good word for the Shrike — he does devour grasshoppers. To bird-lovers, however, this is counterbalanced by his conduct in murdering many small birds. Putting the mildest construction on his behavior, he is undoubtedly a

SOUTHERN SHRIKE:
"BUTCHER-BIRD"

46

glutton and overbearing. Let another bird capture a nice juicy grasshopper and the butcher will chase him around and around, trying to take his dinner.

Alas, one of our most colorful birds must be classed with those that are guilty of abominable practices. The beautiful Blue Jay is a heartless nest-robber. In spring he goes from nest to nest and devours every egg he can find. And I have seen him take a baby bird, hold it down with his foot, and proceed to pick out its brains. He seems to favor the eggs and young of some of our finest singers, such as the Wood Thrush, Mockingbird and Brown Thrasher. The Blue Jay has been accused of catching newly-hatched chicks, but I have not been an eyewitness to this. But those who want songbirds will simply have to hold down the Blue Jay population. They can be trapped and carried to distant wildwoods.

The greatest destroyer of songbirds is the Coopers Hawk. Because of his swiftness and boldness, country people call him "Blue Darter." And a darter he is. He can swoop down almost at one's feet and pick up a little chicken. One day I saw my birds rush madly away from the feeding stations, so I watched to discover the cause of the panic. In a minute a Blue Darter came sailing down the road, about six feet above the ground. No doubt he had been picking up a bird in this way almost every day. His favorite method, however, is to hide in a tree, then dive bomb a bird beneath with incredible swiftness. The Sharp-shinned Hawk also destroys birds.

Let's not confuse this ruthless murderer with our beautiful and harmless little Sparrow Hawk. Just because it is named "Hawk," this beneficial species is almost gone. It is a good deal smaller than the Coopers Hawk and much more brightly colored. Every effort should be made to protect this vanishing species which was once so plentiful and which could be heard calling "Killi-killi-killi" as it circled over fields in search of grasshoppers. What a pity it had not been called "Grasshopper Hawk!"

MEADOWLARK: SUMMER SINGER

There is an eastern and a western Meadowlark, and the latter is said to have a finer song than the eastern species. If this is true it must be lovely indeed.

Ours has a simple song, but piercingly sweet, and it always reminds me of the opening bar of Dvorak's "Souvenir." His favorite perch is atop a fence-post along the roadside, and it is a pity that cars travel so fast that the occupants cannot enjoy this cheery lay.

The two species look very much alike, a stubby short-tailed bird, but with beautiful markings. His yellow breast and black necktie are conspicuous, and the brown spots and streaks of head and back are harmonious and attractive. In general, the western Meadowlark is found from Texas west, while the other species occupies the area east of Texas. One

MEADOWLARK.
(Adapted from painting by L. A. Fuertes)

or the other of the two species may be found in almost every part of the United States at some season of the year. In winter they congregate in large flocks, and country boys call them "Fieldlarks." They used to be shot for food until they were declared songbirds and protected by law.

They are birds of open fields, as their name would indicate, and are almost never seen in wooded areas. As hill farms are almost a thing of the past, Meadowlarks are most often seen now in riverbottom land, where they can find grasshoppers, boll weevils and other injurious creatures which constitute their food. Farmers should make every effort to encourage and protect them. They also eat grass and weed seeds.

In winter western Meadowlarks come over into Northwest Louisiana and mingle with the flocks of eastern species. At that time they are practically indistinguishable. Both birds are about ten inches long.

Nests of Meadowlarks are hard to find, for they are built in tall grasses which are bent and woven to form a sort of roof. The eggs are white with brown freckles.

FOUR-AND-TWENTY BLACKBIRDS

Of course there are not four-and-twenty species, but there are several kinds of Blackbird. Some people think when they say "Blackbird" they have said it, but this is not so, for there are many variations.

Even the detested Cowbird belongs to the group, but she is a disgrace to the family. Too lazy to build a house for herself, she slips about, laying her eggs in other birds' nests. These deluded little birds hatch and rear these monsters which soon push the rightful heirs out of the nest. Our Cowbird is a rusty black, with a brown head, and is

RED-WINGED
BLACKBIRD

the smallest of the Blackbirds. It has an unpleasant whiny note. I feel sure the honest Blackbirds turn up their beaks at her!

Purple Grackle is the king of the family and steps about with a lordly air. When seen on the ground he is beautiful, for his shining black coat is iridescent in the sun, especially about the head which flashes with green and

purple. Grackles are very gregarious, and in the winter
hundreds will descend on a forest where they hope to find
food until the tops of trees are blackened. Their notes have
an odd mechanical sound like the twisting of a metal toy,
but in chorus it is rather musical. Grackles soon strip a
tree of every berry. In town where water and laurel oaks
are planted they are welcome, for they clean up the drifts of
acorns.

Boat-tailed Grackle is several inches longer than Purple Grackle, but not as attractive as his smaller relative.
He is not as iridescent and his tail is so tremendous one
wonders why it does not weigh him down. Purple Grackle
is about a foot long, but this fellow must be sixteen inches
in length — mostly tail! He is a habitant of the Gulf Coast
country, but is occasionally seen in swamps in the northern
parts of the state.

In winter flocks of Brewer's Blackbird are quite common. This and Rusty Blackbird are much smaller than the
preceding, only eight or nine inches long. Brewer's is quite
handsome, with an iridescent black coat.Rusty, as his name
would indicate, lacks this iridescence, and is less attractive.
His mate would never be taken for a blackbird, for she is
striped with brown, something like a Wren. This species
too is a winter resident.

The prettiest of the family is Redwing, a fairly small
Blackbird with scarlet epaulets edged in yellow. His wife
too is striped with brown and would not be recognized as
the mate of her gaudy husband. His song consists of only
three notes, but they are very musical. All Blackbirds gather
by the thousands in the rice fields in South Louisiana and
are considered a nuisance.

Yellow-headed Blackbird is the most exotic looking
member of the family. About the size of a robin, he is
black, with a brilliant yellow head and upper breast. We
seldom see this pretty fellow, for he just passes through in
migration. But he is one of the many charming species
that make bird-watching exciting in spring.

THE BEAUTIFUL VISITORS

The birds that stay with us the year around hold first place in our affections, but the rare ones who visit us during migratory season are very exciting. I shall never forget the first time I saw a Rose-breasted Grosbeak. I heard a new note in the bird chorus, ran to see, and there just outside my kitchen window sat this beautiful creature. He was facing me, so that his bright rose breast was much in evidence. He is about the size of his cousin, the Cardinal. Except for the brilliant patch of color on his breast, he is smartly dressed in black and white. This lovely bird is usually seen in Louisiana the latter part of April and early May.

So far as I know the Scarlet Tanager has honored me with his presence only once. The red of his coat is so brilliant as to make our Summer Tanager look dull. As an added touch his wings are black. As he flits about searching for food he is like a flame among the trees. Scarlet Tanagers stop with us briefly, then go farther

GOLDFINCH
Like a bright-yellow Flower among the grass.

north — some to Canada — to nest. When he comes back through in fall this gay fellow probably will not be recognized, for he will have changed his suit to one of dull olive.

One day in spring I drove up in front of my house when a whole flock of Gold Finches flew up from the ground. I stopped my car and sat breathless. In a very few minutes they came back down and went on feeding on grass seeds. It looked as if someone had scattered bright-yellow flowers over the ground. Their color is purest aureolin, seldom as beautiful in paintings as it really is, and their little black wings form a striking contrast. But, like the Scarlet Tanager, he dons a sober coat in fall and is difficult to recognize when he comes back from his northern nesting grounds. This little Finch has an exquisite song which I had the pleasure of hearing in North Alabama. How I wish these dainty creatures would stay with me!

When late April comes bird watchers go slowly mad, trying to identify the many Warblers passing through. There are so many species, and many so much alike, identification is difficult. Some are strikingly beautiful and easily recognized. Two of the loveliest stay with us all the year, but are seldom seen. These are the Redstart and Prothonotary Warbler who live near lakes and big streams. The Prothonotary has been known to nest in boxes and buildings by the side of lakes.

When I hear unusual notes at this time I drop everything, snatch a bird book and go out and sit still in shrubbery. Migratory Warblers usually travel in flocks, often a number of species together. They are so hungry and so busy feeding on insects they pay little heed to the watcher and come quite close. Some are so brightly colored they are easily recognized. The veriest amateur can identify the Bay-breasted, Magnolia, Black-throated Green, etc. These little visitors constitute a fascinating study.

WHIP-POOR-WILL CLAN
BIRD WORLD'S "BIGMOUTHS"

When people in North Louisiana say "Whip-poor-will," they are more than likely referring to the Chuck-will's-widow, for the true Whip-poor-will tarries with us only briefly. Some books state that this bird breeds in this area, but George Lowery ("Louisiana Birds") says there is no record of their doing so.

For a night or two in April I hear his clean-cut, distinctive "whip-poor-will" repeated over and over, then no more.

Some persons have the idea that Whip-poor-will, Chuck-will's-wodow and Night-hawk are one and the same bird. As a matter of fact they are three different species, though of course all belong to the same family. They are strange birds, and their family name, Goat-suckers, is even stranger. This arose from the fact that peasants in Europe thought the species native there robbed the goats of their milk! They do have most unbird-like mouths and they would be seen swooping about the goats in late evening — of course catching insects on the wing.

CHUCK-WILL'S-WIDOW
(adapted from a drawing by R. I. Brasher)

Our own old Chuck-will's-widow is the largest of the group, almost a foot long. About half of his big head is split to form his outrageous mouth — the true beak being tiny. He is modestly colored, simulating the dead leaves on which he sits — the mingled brown, black and white being almost indistinguishable from his surroundings. Even the eggs are dappled like the earth on which they rest, and a good thing, for the parents make no pretense of a nest. If you should happen to frighten one from the eggs, don't follow the bird, for it will flap and stagger about to draw the intruder away. Great care must be taken or one will step on the two eggs.

His notes are so distinctive they have given him his name, Chuck-will's-widow. The sandhill interpretation is even more descriptive, "chip-fell-out-o-the-white-oak," accent on first and last words. At dusk, and even after nightfall, his call will be heard from nearby woods, sometimes so rapidly repeated and so endlessly it is a wonder he does not fall over from lack of breath. There is something very attractive about this call and I begin listening for it in mid-April. This year it came on April 16.

Usually the Whip-poor-will is heard a few days earlier. This is a smaller bird, a little over nine inches long, with much the same coloring as the preceding. Their habits are quite similar, and both have the enormous mouths for catching insects on the wing.

The same is true of the Night-hawk, in size between the two already discussed — about ten inches. But there is one difference; while the first two are almost never seen, the Night-hawk stages quite a display after sunset. As a child I loved to sit in an open meadow and watch the graceful swoopings of these birds as they caught mosquitoes and other winged creatures from the air. If one is quite still they will dive very near one's head. As they swoop, big mouths wide open, the wind through wing-feathers makes a loud "zoom," and presumably this gave the bird its other common name, "Bull-bat." Both his names are almost as ridiculous as Goat-sucker, for he resembles neither a hawk nor a bat, and it takes a bit of imagination to think that his "zoom" sounds like the bellow of a bull.

All three of these birds are valuable citizens, as they devour quantities of mosquitoes and other winged pests. As they are non-perching species, they have tiny feet, and that is why they always sit on ground or rooftop and are never seen in trees.

SPARE THE OWLS

Just cry "Owl!" or "Hawk!" and men reach for their guns. Now that we are so much better enlightened in regard to the balance of nature, it does look as if this indiscriminate slaughter would cease. The rhythm in the increase and decrease of Snowy Owl and the Lemming in the Arctic is amazing and beautiful.

Owls do their hunting at night and thus destroy innumerable rats, mice, rabbits, gophers and other rodents. Where the Owls have been killed off these pests increase rapidly and take over, causing an immense amount of damage.

The Great Horned Owl, the king of the family, is about two feet in length. With his upright "ears" and big round eyes he somewhat resembles a cat, so is sometimes called "Cat Owl." He favors swamps and heavy woodlands, but his deep solemn "hoo-hoo, hoo hoo-hoo" may be heard for quite a distance. His call is full of dignity, entirely different from the roistering yells of the "Hoot Owl." Where farmers allow their chickens to roost in trees the Great Horned will occasionally pick him off one. But I

GREAT HORNED OWL
(Adapted from photographs)

would rather shut my chickens up at night — and keep my Owl.

Next in size is the Barred Owl, beautifully marked, but without "ears." Almost everyone is familiar with his usual call, "Who cooks, who cooks, who cooks for you-all!" but he is the clown of the family and has a fairly full repertoire. His loud "whah-ha-ha, whah hoo-ah," repeated with variations, sounds like demoniacal laughter. I have never known whether there are just one or two indulging in this performance, but it sounds like a dozen! He can also let out a panther-like scream which, when heard right overhead, can chill the blood. He too will snatch an occasional chicken, if temptingly exposed. Unlike those of other Owls, his big eyes are so dark as to seem black.

Once a neighbor said, "I wish you would go with me to the Regions and see what that strange bird is." When he told me they caught it in their barn I had my suspicions. Sure enough, it was a Barn Owl, so different from others of the family that once seen is never forgotten. A slender, light-colored bird, it has unusually long legs and is about seventeen inches tall. It has a white, long heart shaped face, sharply outlined in dark brown. A ridge of feathers forms a long "nose." The face is so much like that of a monkey it is often called "Monkey-faced Owl." Lucky is the farmer whose barn is occupied by a pair of these odd creatures, for they will keep it completely free of mice and rats. The books say it makes a hissing sound, but a friend who has had a pair in his barn says it is quite unlike a hiss. To him it sounds more like a squeal of a rabbit that has been caught.

The person who named the Screech Owl should be sued for libel. The little fellow's cry bears no resemblance to a "screech," but is a soft, sad, quavering wail. An old myth that it is a sign of death causes superstitious folk to turn a shoe upside down or turn a sock! Many persons say it "gives them the creeps," but when one realizes it is a love-song it is more acceptable. One night on a camping trip I became charmed with Screech Owls. I heard odd low little sounds and stepped out into the bright moonlight. There on a long horizontal branch of a tree two of these little birds were doing a ceremonial dance. They would face each other and bow elaborately. Then they would back off, bow again and repeat.

When protecting their young, however, Screech Owls are definitely NOT gentle. Once I had placed a section of hollow tree up in a big hickory for the squirrels. A pair of Screech Owls said "thank you," and moved in. I had never seen their eggs, so when I judged the time to be right I had a ladder placed against the tree and climbed up. But I had waited too long. Instead of eggs, there were two soft balls of white "fur." I HAD to have a picture of them, so I went down for my camera. When I climbed up again there sat Papa and Mama making queer little noises. I ignored them and put my hand in the nest to move the babies into the light. I saw nothing, but felt a sharp slash on my wrist and blood began to run. I decided it was not really necessary for me to have pictures of baby Screech Owls!

These small birds destroy countless mice, grasshoppers, etc. and do no harm. They nest in hollows, but cannot dig one out, so have to search for holes in trees or for those made by Woodpeckers. When nothing else is available they will occupy a box placed on a tree-trunk.

The numbers of all owls are diminishing, so it behooves us to do what we can to save these valuable birds.

WRENS MARRY ONCE

We have many charming birds, but after many years of association with them I pronounce the Carolina Wren the most winsome. When referring to this little bird I want to say "she" — so dainty-looking, so full of delightful whimsies. Others must have felt this, for there is the old affectionate name, "Jenny Wren".

Winter visitors of the family are tiny House Wren and little stubtailed Winter Wren. But there is no danger of confusing them, for these two are much smaller than Carolina Wren and not so beautifully colored. The latter is a lovely little creature. I think a White-throat Sparrow is richly colored until a Wren lights beside him, when he looks almost dull by contrast. Wren is a bright rufous-brown, breast and side buff with just a flush of the brown. A long sharply-defined stripe over the eye adds a look of distinction.

The Wren could be the symbol of restless energy, never still an instant, bobbing up and down and assuming various poses. To feed this incredible energy he consumes an astonishing number of insects, which makes him valuable as well as lovable. Spiders constitute his favorite "dish" and

CAROLINA WREN

he may be observed going in and out between timbers in buildings searching for these items.

Books on birds usually credit Carolina Wren with one song, "Teakettle, teakettle, teakettle." This always amazes me, for he has so many different songs they are sometimes credited to the Mockingbird. Most often heard is a clear "Witchery, witchery, witchery!" All of his songs are ringing and full of cheer. In spring we hear, "Secret, secret, secret!" perhaps referring to his cunningly concealed nest. This jolly fellow sings for us all through the year. When a bitter wind was blowing and snow falling I have seen him perch on a twig and pour forth his bubbling song, "Cheerily, cheerily, cheerily!" giving a lift to the heart. He has a call which can only be spelled "kewp", which is almost ear-splitting when heard very near. How can such a volume of sound come from so small a throat!

Some time ago I saw an item in Ripley's column to the effect that the male Wren often builds several nests and *has a wife in each.* What a slanderous untruth! The male Wren does sometimes build several nests, but they are unoccupied, and it is my belief that this is the work of one who has no mate. The truth is the Wren is a model husband who helps build the nest and watches over it while the lady is brooding — occasionally bringing her a delicious katydid. Or he may tuck a soft feather in by her, with many loving twitters. Most amazing of all, Wrens stay mated. There is a little white-oak basket swung under my porch roof and every spring Mr. and Mrs. Wren rear a brood in it. Then when cold rains begin in fall they come back and sleep in it every night — just Papa and Mama.

So many times friends tell me, "I bought the cutest Wren house, but they won't have it!" I say, "Let me see it." Just as I expected, it is a tiny affair, probably designed for little House Wrens. Carolina Wrens accumulate an astonishing amount of leaves and straw, then construct their nest in this, with the entrance at one side. To accommodate a Carolina Wren's nest, a box should be about eight inches

square and ten inches deep. The opening should be small —
to keep out intruders — about the size of a fifty-cent piece.
They will also make their homes in big gourds and in des-
peration will build in a man's overcoat pocket or an old boot.

The most amazing choice of a home was in my car,
where it was parked in front of the door. They found an
inaccessible spot under the hood — the garage man could
not locate it — so there was nothing to do but let matters
take their course. When I had to go to the grocery store I
would say, "Please hurry! My baby Wrens will get hungry."
(Happily, the groceryman knew me and my "queer" ways!)
When the engine started Mama flew out and perched on a
dogwood tree till my return. I was very dubious about the
outcome of such proceedings, but one happy day little Wrens
erupted from the car — as healthy as if reared in more
suitable surroundings.

Good rich cornbread will bring Wrens to the feeder,
for they must have protein. In a retaining wall below my
window there are big rocks, with little holes and crevices,
and into these I stuff cornbread. The Wrens dig this out
with their long sharp bills, while the big-beaked Finches
cannot reach it. Any effort is well worthwhile that will
bring these delightful little creatures close to our homes.

LARGE WOODPECKERS GETTING SCARCE

The Ivory-bill is the largest of all Woodpeckers, but, alas, it is supposed to be gone — along with the Passenger Pigeon. But we still hope there may be a few left in some remote swamp. The Pileated Woodpecker is almost as large and almost identical in appearance, except the bill is black instead of white. There is no mistaking this bird, for he is as large as a Leghorn hen, with a black and white coat and a brilliant red cockade.

The Pileated is becoming rare and should be rigidly protected. The main factor that has contributed to the disappearance of these two large birds is the fact that they

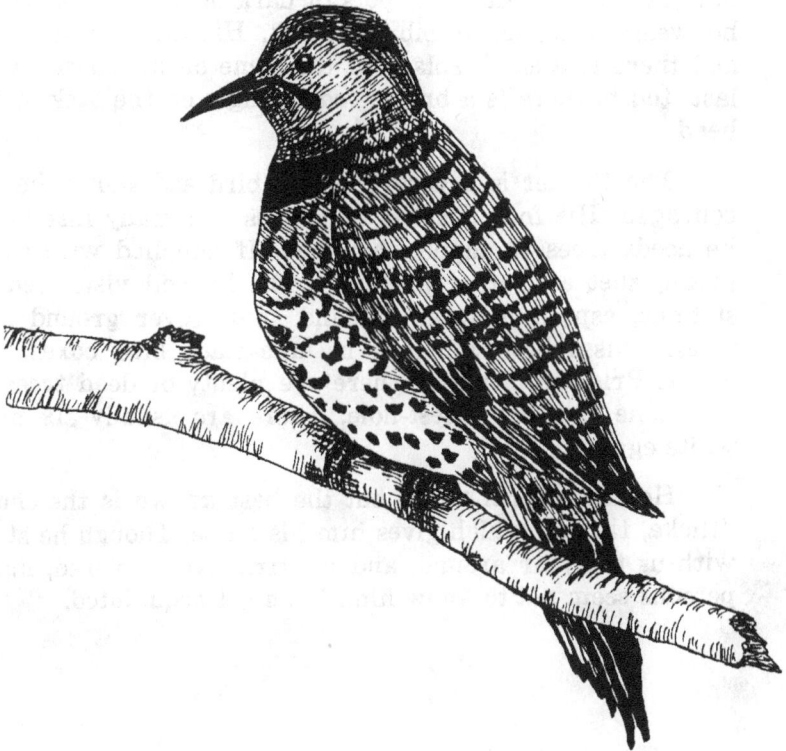

FLICKER: YELLOW-HAMMER.

feed on the big beetles and their larvae found in dead and dying trees. So the best place to look for them is in undisturbed forests. The Pileated lives in my Briarwood forest, and I am often startled by his strident note, which can be heard for a long distance. An odd characteristic is that they often make holes in living trees in which to nest, chiseling them out smoothly with their powerful beaks.

The Flicker, better known here as the Yellow-hammer, is a handsome fellow, thirteen inches long. His attractive coloring is quite conspicuous. His back and wings are soft brown with irregular rows of small black spots. His breast is light yellow with little spots of dark brown, and in front he wears a collar, or bib, of black. His tail is also black and there is a small splash of the same on his cheek. As a last touch, there is a bright red triangle on the back of his head.

The Flicker is a very valuable bird and should be encouraged. His food consists of beetles and many insects, so he needs trees to supply this food. If supplied with cornbread, suet and other protein foods, he will visit feeding stations, especially when ice and snow cover ground and trees. This fellow will nest in man-made bird boxes, but not at Briarwood, where there are plenty of dead trees in which he can dig a nest-hole. There are usually six pure white eggs.

He has several notes, but the best known is the sharp "flicka, flicka," which gives him his name. Though he stays with us the year around, and is attractively colored, many persons seem not to know him. Let's get acquainted.

THE LESSER WOODPECKERS

The largest of this group is the Red-bellied Woodpecker. It does seem that this handsome bird might have been given a more respectable name, especially as it is misleading. He has no red underneath, while the entire top of his head is blazing scarlet. The back and upper part of wings are marked with zebra stripes of black and white. This species is with us the year around, and with his size — about ten inches — and bright coloring should be better known.

Next in size comes our dear old Redhead, a valuable bird, but no longer common, because of trigger-happy, unthinking persons. He is easily recognized by his black and white coat (no bars), and entire head of bright red. He used to be seen in towns. At my old home in Arcadia I used to watch him turning somersaults in mid-air, catching insects on the wing. The public must be aroused as to the necessity for his protection, or this fine bird will go to join the Passenger Pigeon.

The ones who named our birds had a special gift for misnomers. The Red-cockaded Woodpecker has *no* cockade! His black-white coloring is much like that of the Red-bellied, but the red on top of head is lacking. It is black instead, with a tiny line of red, almost invisible. The zebra marking of the two is quite similar, but this bird is nearly two inches shorter than the former.

The Sapsucker is a pretty fellow, conspicuously marked with black and white and with red on top of his head and under his chin. The upper part of the breast is faintly washed with yellow. I hate to tattle, but this is the least desirable of the tribe. He has the strange habit of pecking holes in living trees, his strong beak penetrating to the cambium layer of bark and causing sap to flow. He then returns to sip this sap and also to eat small insects caught in the sticky fluid. Now I have seen it claimed that this does no harm, but that is a mistake. He favors all species of Eleagnus, and every year I have several branches killed

DOWNY WOODPECKER, The smallest of the family.

by being completely girdled. But his favorite tree is the apple. Fortunately, he rings the upper part of fairly large trees which do not seem to suffer from his work. The sap which exudes is quite sweet — when a child I sampled it! Then why does he girdle Yellow Jessamine vines, which are bitter? He sometimes kills these. Like all of the tribe, this species destroys injurious insects — but I can do without him. He is quite "tame" and is so greedy he gobbles up the food from small birds.

More misnomers: Hairy and Downy Woodpeckers are neither hairy nor downy, but have feathers just as do all other species. An odd thing is that the two birds are almost exactly alike, except that Downy is nearly three inches smaller than Hairy. Both are sharply marked black and white with broken bars on the wings and a red spot on the back of the head. Downy is the smallest of all our Woodpeckers, only six or seven inches long. He is a shy little fellow, creeping up tree-trunks in search of eggs and larvae of insects.

All of our Woodpeckers nest in holes in trees, so if one wants the valuable birds, a few dead trees should be left to afford them homes. This is why they are more commonly seen in woodlands of some size. All lay three to six white eggs and, if not disturbed, multiply satisfactorily. There is no reason why these fine birds should disappear.

THE REDHEAD IS GOING, GOING

The Red-headed Woodpecker will soon be gone unless we take drastic action to save this valuable bird. He is such a showy fellow, it seems strange that so few persons have observed his passing. With his white vest, blue-black coat and brilliant red head, he is very conspicuous. He has no song, only the usual Woodpecker calls, but he is of inestimable value in destroying harmful insects.

In the last report of the Louisiana Ornithological Society there was this startling statement: "Interesting was the total absence of the Red-headed Woodpecker, a species reported by seven of the eight parties last year!" An alarming decrease in just one year!

Contributing causes of his disappearance are the removal of nesting sites and food sources. In the old days of "deadening" trees — girdling them — to make way for cultivation, the resulting dead stumps supplied the beetles and grubs on which he fed and also gave him the places he needed to make nests. This bird pecks holes in dead trees, in the bottom of which he places his home. Nesting boxes do not tempt him — at least I have never seen one nest in a box. If you really want to attract the Redhead get a section of dead tree-trunk and set it up on your grounds. It should be at least fifteen feet high.

The Redhead — unlike his big cousins, the Pileated and Ivorybill Woodpeckers — is a friendly fellow and will come to the feeding station. The last one I had came and ate cornbread every day, with me standing within a few feet of him. I could even call him, "Come on, Red!" and in a few minutes he would appear.

The wretched Starlings drive him away from his nesting sites. Dead and dying trees which supply food and homes are almost gone. But the biggest contributing factor in his disappearance may be summed up in one word — guns. Alas, that beautiful red head makes a perfect target!

An old man told me, "My eyes must still be pretty good.

RED-HEADED WOODPECKER

I killed a Redhead with a .22 rifle." I said, "Well, you may have got the last one!" A younger man, and a highly intelligent one, was shooting them several years ago. When I protested, he said, "Why, the telephone people ask us to kill them." How outrageous! If a Redhead pecks a hole in a telephone pole it is because there is already a rotten spot there.

At Christmas parents supply every boy with a gun — but fail to teach him what NOT to shoot. Boys kill songbirds indiscriminately, even during the nesting season when baby birds are left to starve. Parents, are you on the job? There is supposed to be no shooting in my woods, but now and then a youngster slips in with his .22 (thinking the sound will not carry), so I feel sure that is what became of my "Old Red."

We have saved the Whooping Cranes from extermination, but lost the spectacular Ivory-billed Woodpecker. Shall we let the valuable Redhead follow? In times past, he was one of our commonest birds. I used to love to watch him tumbling in mid-air, catching insects on the wing. But now — when have you seen a Redhead?

BIRD BUNCOMBE
It Just Isn't So!

Our Yellow-billed Cuckoo — "Raincrow" to us — is a much maligned bird. Because the English Cuckoo has the sneaky habit of laying its eggs in the nests of other birds our good old Raincrow has been accused of the same practice. Well, it just isn't so! During my life I have found many of their nests with their own two blue eggs therein. He is a sloppy home-maker, it must be admitted, for the nest is merely a handful of twigs thrown together, and one wonders why the eggs don't fall through.

The truth about this fellow is strange enough. The most peculiar fact is that the two big eggs are seldom exactly the same size and shape! This is a common bird, but so shy he is seldom seen. He slips about among trees, flying rather uncertainly, as if not quite sure as to what he wants to do. In wooded areas, they often build their nests near dwellings, only a few feet above the ground. Their call is unmistakable, a series of guttural notes, "cuc cuc cuc" — repeated rapidly — and ending with three "cuckoos". This requires close listening, for the first syllable is barely discernible. The folk belief is that if an owl hoots in the daytime or the Raincrow calls at night it is going to rain. Hence its common name. This is a friend to be encouraged, for his diet consists almost entirely of insects, among which is the disgusting tent caterpillar.

Another maligned friend is the lovable Catbird. He is accused of eating the eggs of other birds, but never in my long life have I caught him in the act. So I simply don't believe it! An astonishing number of persons think his only note is the catlike mew which gives him his name. How sad! His song is soft, sweet and varied, but for some reason he hides when singing, so the show-off Mockingbird gets credit for his performance. When you hear a song in spring which is much like that of Mockingbird, but softer, slip around and peer among the trees and you will see a

71

trim fellow in Quaker gray, with a few white markings
— Catbird.

It has been stated by ornithologists that the male bird
"stakes out his claim" in nesting season, allowing no other
bird to enter there, and sings for this reason *only*. This
theory caught the popular fancy and has repeatedly appeared in print. Well, perhaps this condition exists in
small areas where nesting sites are limited, but here at
Briarwood where there is room for all it just does not
happen this way. Once I read a dramatic story about a
Cardinal being thus shut off from his favorite source of
food, the intimation being that he would starve rather
than encroach on his neighbor's domain. Nonsense! My
numerous Cardinals feed together and build their nests
not many feet apart with no apparent rivalry. Of course an
occasional male chases another, but this happens at any

RAINCROW: YELLOW-BILLED CUCKOO.
(Adapted from painting by L. A. Fuertes)

time of year, as they are rather pugnacious. If birds sing only to "stake out their claims" for breeding grounds, why do they sing in fall? Mockingbirds pour out their sweetest songs at that time. Wrens and Cardinals sing all during winter.

If bird lovers would observe for themselves and not just repeat what they read, we would get at the truth about our feathered friends.

BOBWHITE, SONGBIRD

No, the Bobwhite is not classed as a songbird, but I never see a family cross the road in front of my car that I don't say, "Oh, you pretty things! I wish you were not so good to eat." But I suppose the hunter would shoot them anyway, even if they were not delicious; for when a covey thunders up in front of his gun pulling the trigger is reflex action.

Like most animals and birds, they are not afraid of cars, and mother will run across with a whole family of babies twinkling along behind her all in line.

Who does not love the male's clear ringing "bobwhite!", the very essence of the summer morning? The mating call is a much softer note and their "talk" consists of rapidly repeated very low sounds. Bobwhite is a ventriloquist, and it is difficult to locate the softer calls. When I used to write at a little one-room cabin right in the woods, I became intimately acquainted with Quails. The house was built of brown logs and the birds thought it was just part of the woods. Wrens would look in the door and scold for being an intruder! Quails brought their families, "talked" right under my window, wallowed in the sand in protected spots and jumped to pick the deerberries growing all about.

The Bobwhite is a faithful father and helps rear the children. He and his wife often nested at the back of the garden, where there were plenty of juicy insects. One summer day I was lying in a hammock on the back porch when I was startled by a loud "bobwhite!" There was Papa, perched on the topmost twig of a crape myrtle. He looked warily about, then gave the "all-clear" signal. Up stepped Mama, with seven small children behind her! Then Papa came down, and they all ate bread crumbs around the steps. After that they repeated this performance every day, and of course I scattered extra crumbs for them.

A Quail nest is a beautiful piece of architecture hid-

74

BOBWHITE QUAIL

den beneath a thick pine bush with tall grass all around. This is bent and arched over to form a room, so that the nest is practically invisible to the passerby. As a child at Arcadia, I once found a nest with twenty white eggs — a sight I have never forgotten. The next day when I took my brother to see it, the mother would not stir. Quietly watching, we presently saw a tiny head peep out from Mother's feathers! The next day they were gone, for babies can run as soon as hatched.

When I was walking at the edge of a field one summer day, a mother Quail flopped in front of me. I stepped up to see how badly she was hurt, but she fluttered just out of reach, and then it dawned on me that she was trying to draw me away from her young. Looking down, I could see nothing. Not until I got on hands and knees and parted dead grasses could I distinguish the perfectly camouflaged little creatures from their surroundings. You don't believe birds can talk? Then watch a mother Quail and her brood. At the first alarm she gives a low note and her children drop, to lie motionless until Mother says "rise and run."

Quails like all sorts of peas, wild and cultivated, and Lespedeza bicolor attracts them. In winter, they will come near a dwelling to feast on chops, cornbread and sunflower seed. They are lovely and valuable friends.

THE SPARROW HAWK, VANISHING SPECIES

The Sparrow Hawk is a true Falcon, closely related to the famous hunting Hawks of Europe and Asia. What a pity this beautiful bird was called a "Hawk," for to be so designated was to invite the guns of hunters. It is one of the most beneficial species of birds, feeding almost entirely on mice, small snakes, grasshoppers and many insects. It is a denizen of open fields, where its chosen food abounds. There, perched on a dead snag, it becomes an easy target.

The fact that hill farms are almost a thing of the past has hastened the decline of these charming birds. It is interesting to observe that conditions fifty years ago favored their prospering. In those days farmers wishing to clear new fields "deadened" the trees, cutting the bark around the trunks. These decaying trunks offered perfect sites for nests of Woodpeckers, who excavated holes. Later, these might be occupied by Bluebirds, Screech Owls and Sparrow Hawks. Also, dead and dying trees supplied numerous grubs and burrowing insects.

This species is the smallest of the Hawks. Even with its unusually long tail it measures only ten inches. Its coloring is exquisite: the top of its head deep blue-gray; wings and tip of tail even darker; back and tail rich rufous-brown; breast fawn-colored with dark-brown spots. The head has striking touches of black. When on the wing it cries "killi, killi, killi," and country children call it "Killi-hawk."

These gentle creatures are very intelligent and easily tamed. Boys used to catch them while young and make pets of them.

Unlike other Hawks, this little Falcon makes its nest in a natural hollow or one excavated by one of the numerous Woodpeckers. It is stated that it will build in a nesting box, but I have not known this to happen. The four or five eggs are creamy-white, variously spotted,

77

SPARROW HAWK
(Adapted from a painting by L. A. Fuertes)

speckled or splashed with dark red and brown.

The man with a gun seems to consider any Hawk legitimate prey, which is most unfortunate, when only two species are very destructive of bird life. The "Little Blue-darter," (Coopers hawk), and the "Big Blue-darter" (Sharp-shinned Hawk), are so swift and bold they can and will snatch up a little chicken at one's feet. They are death to small birds, for they hide, then dart and disappear in a flash. The Goshawk is very destructive of poultry, but happily for us it is a denizen of the far north.

Probably the most-slaughtered of all is the beautiful big Red-tailed Hawk, often seen sailing in the summer sky. It is even called, mistakenly, "Hen-hawk," but it has been proven that its diet consists almost entirely of rodents, snakes, grasshoppers, etc. Only in extreme hunger does it attack poultry. Thus it behooves farmers to protect this largest of our Hawks and the lovely little Sparrow Hawk, the smallest.

FAMILY BIRDS

It is commonly believed that birds scatter when they leave the nest, but some stay together in family groups till fall and sometimes all winter. Chippy and Field Sparrows may be seen feeding in small bands of five or six. All our native Sparrows are more or less gregarious and in winter gather in flocks. This is true of Meadow Larks too.

Young Titmice and Chickadees remain with the parents for a long time, five or six coming together to feeding stations. But they are very mannerly, one at a time seizing a crumb, then making way for another.

Bluebirds keep together in family groups till spring. Alas, they will not come to feeding stations, but one can see five or six strung out along telephone wires. And when everything is frozen up in very cold weather they come in

PAPA CARDINAL FEEDS HIS CHILD

to drink from water that is kept thawed.

Quails rear large families. I found a nest once with twenty eggs — a beautiful sight. It was in sedge-grass under a pine bush, and the nest had walls and was partially roofed over. Father, mother and the children make up a covey, sometimes large, sometimes small. The covey does not break up till mating time in spring. Baby Quails can run as soon as hatched, but as they stay on the ground their numbers are greatly reduced by snakes, foxes, 'possums, etc.

As a family man the male Cardinal deserves the highest award. While the female is brooding he brings her food. Then when the young are hatched he works as hard as the mother at keeping their greedy mouths filled. But after the babies are grown in size he outdoes the female in the matter of baby-sitting. With food right at his feet a full-grown youngster will approach a parent, begging to be fed. With wings quivering in the most infantile manner he approaches mama. But she says "no, you lazy scamp! I've done my part — now you get your own food." So he goes to the male, and this indulgent papa picks up a crumb and feeds it to the spoiled brat!

Sometimes other birds are as indulgent. The other day, to my surprise, I saw a Pine Warbler feeding a child as large as itself. And I have seen a poor little Vireo giving food to an imposter Cowbird-child much larger than the imposed-on parent.

Of course wild Geese and Ducks remain in family flocks. A V-formation flying south is usually made up of the parents with that year's "hatch", the brave old father leading his children on their first great adventure.

THE PARTY AT THE BIRDBATH

One day last spring I happened to look out and there, perched on the birdbath, was a beautiful Rose-breasted Grosbeak. This was only the second time I had ever seen one at Briarwood. Later on the same day I spied a pair of them in low trees near the house. They pass through in a

REDSTARTS AT BIRD-BATH

migratory season, but tarry only a few hours.

In late summer I was sitting on the back porch when a fluttering at the birdbath attracted my attention. There were three birds in it. They began lifting their wings and spreading their tails, and thus identified themselves — Redstarts. So far as I know, no other bird exhibits these dainty butterfly-like motions. They were all females or immature young, for the broad bands on wings and tails were light yellow. Males display bright orange-red. So I decided the group consisted of a mother and three children. The exciting part was that I had never before seen a Redstart at Briarwood! They were not sending up geysers of water as do the White-throats, but were having a whale of a time nevertheless. Where did they come from? The nearest I had ever observed these beautiful little creatures was at Black Lake, twelve miles away. I have not seen one here since, so evidently they were just passing through and were attracted by the shine of water.

Big old Brown Thrashers splash so enthusiastically they throw all the water out of the little pool. Sometimes a Wren gets so carried away she SWIMS across two or three times. Chickadees become so infatuated they just can't get enough of bathing. One will get wet all over, then fly up to a twig to preen. But he looks down and says, "I must have just one more dip!" Then in he goes again.

During the fall it was dry and warm and insects so plentiful that Titmice and Chickadees scorned my cornbread. I had not seen one in weeks. Then one day they gave a swimming party. I don't know just who received invitations, but every Titmouse and Chickadee must have attended. They seem to know they are related and are often seen together. The winter huckleberry that hangs overhead was filled with them, but they were very mannerly and each waited his turn. One splashed merrily, then flew up on a twig to preen while another took his turn.

My birdbath is a crude affair which a schoolboy and I made, but nothing affords me so much pleasure. We built

up a circular wall of native rocks and cement about thirty
inches high. This was filled in with soil, leaving a bowl-
shaped depression at the top. A lining of cement finished
the job. While this was soft I pressed some large pebbles
into it, for it frightens birds if their feet slip. The happy
splashing continues till almost dark, summer and winter.
I have seen them bathing when there was ice in the water.
When this facility is not available to birds they are de-
prived of something which seems necessary to their comfort
and happiness.

AUTUMN SONGS

Few persons seem to observe that the Mockingbird, our most famous singer, gives us his sweetest songs in autumn. In spring he is fiercely competitive, imitating other birds as if in derision.

In September we hear none of these harsh sounds. He sings soft gentle melodies as if thinking of lovely memories.

The Mockingbird is a conscious performer and loves attention and appreciation. When he sings a tentative note or two, tell him, "How sweet! But sing some more." He will turn his head as if listening, then give forth with several bars. Talk to him again, telling him how beautifully he sings. Then he will lift his head and pour out an exquisite series of varied notes. But always he sings softly, as if he might be rehearsing. In fact, one has to be rather near to get the full benefit of his performance.

In the Gulf Coast region, where flowers bloom all winter, the Mockingbird never stops singing. But in our area one hears him only on unusually warm, spring-like days.

Indians are keen observers. The Choctaw name for Mockingbird means "bird of many tongues".

Papa Cardinal is beginning to look rather dapper again, but he is still too shy to sing. Seldom do we hear his bright voice until about the middle of December. Then on mild sunny days he will surprise us with his beautiful spring song. The same thing is true in January.

Occasionally we hear the Red-eyed Vireo "talking," but he does not keep up a continuous chatter as he does all summer. The more musical White-eye is silent — probably he has already left us.

Now and then the little Wren gives us one of his gay rollicking songs — he has many. Of course he is not singing constantly now as he did in spring and early summer.

MOCKINGBIRD

Perhaps he is giving these as a pattern to the children, for all during September young Wrens are learning to sing. The songs are imperfect, with many broken notes, but easily recognized by those familiar with the family melodies.

Why are all the birds so preoccupied at this time? My theory is that the abundant insect life keeps them busy, for most all birds relish these tidbits. They are very indifferent to the feeding stations, only the greedy Jays never failing to appear. I always worry a little when so many of my favorites are absent at roll call. But now the little Sparrows are beginning to come in — I had a whole flock of Field and Chippy Sparrows. But not till late October will the White-throats return.

NAMING THE BIRDS

Mention Flicker and the average country boy will not know what you are talking about. Say "Yellow-hammer" and he will understand, for that is the common name for this handsome big Woodpecker. This is also true of Shrike, for "Butcher-bird" is the name by which he is best known. It is a fitting one, from his revolting habit of impaling small birds on thorns and barb wire.

In the case of Kingbird, the "book name" is more appropriate than the common one, "Bee-martin". Ornithologists say he eats few bees, but, being a Flycatcher, he destroys insects on the wing. His bravery deserves the title, Kingbird. I have seen him riding on the back of a Hawk, meanwhile pecking it viciously on the head. It is amusing to watch the bird diving and twisting in an effort to dislodge the small one! Any intruder that comes near his nest will receive the same treatment.

When the country man hears the odd call of a Cuckoo he says it is going to rain, so this fellow is a "Raincrow". The name "Bullbat" may seem a little far-fetched for the Nighthawk, but he does swoop and dive, bat-like, in late evening. And sit still in an open meadow until he zooms quite near, and the booming sound made by his wings might possibly be called a roar.

Pretty little Sparrow-hawk is called "Killy-hawk" by country boys, because he constantly cries "killy, killy, killy"! So, too, Towhee was given his name in imitation of his call. But here in the South he is better known as "Joree". If the accent is put on the second syllable the name sounds very much like his sharp note.

The handsome Pileated Woodpecker is called "Indian Hen". Strangest of all, he is also known as "Lord God"! This is a corruption of the old name, Log-cock.

In common parlance a Nuthatch is a "Tomtit" and Brown Thrasher is "Thrush". This is understandable, as Thrushes are famous for their singing and Thrasher has

87

KINGBIRD (BEE MARTIN)

a very fine song. Wood Thrush is known as "Swamp Lark", as it loves woodlands near small streams, and its lovely liquid notes suggest gently falling water.

Coopers Hawk is known as "Blue-darter" because of its ability to dart down and snatch up a little chicken right at one's feet. This is the only Hawk I would kill — if I could ever get in gunshot — because I have often seen it catch my beloved songbirds. The big hawks should be spared, as they devour wood rats, gophers and other destructive rodents. Examination of their stomachs has proved that they catch few birds and poultry.

When my brothers and I were children we gave our own names to a number of birds. Kinglets were so tiny there was just one logical title, "Tots". Tufted Titmouse was, of course, "Topknot" and Chickadee was "Black-cap". We were very close observers and so were intrigued by the fact that the Lark Sparrow did not hop — as did all others of the family — but walked or ran. Because of this we dubbed him "Pacer". This beautiful little bird, with his delightful song, has almost vanished. He loved open fields and even made his nest right on the ground beneath a cotton stalk or other plant. Now fields are replaced by dense stands of young pines — hill farms are no more. The ranks of lusty young pines are fine — but I grieve for the lost song of the Lark Sparrow.

AUGUST IS "SILENT TIME"

August is the silent time. Birds are moulting and their voices are stilled. The dapper Cardinal is so dowdy-looking he is embarrassed and we hear nothing from him. Even the faithful Wood Thrushes, who sing all day long, are hiding, their voices hushed. Now and then there is the raucous voice of the Blue Jay and occasionally a little Wren gives us a brief song. This is all — the woods are strangely silent.

But there is one exception. That jewel, the Indigo Bunting, pours out a sprightly gush of melody all through the day which sounds so cool it lifts the burden of extreme

INDIGO BUNTING

heat. Just why it sings so late — almost to the end of August — no one seems to know.

This lovely little creature has other habits just as mysterious. You may have it for several years, then no more. A flock will sometimes stay during early summer, then vanish. They feed on grass seeds and it may be that they are very choosy as to the species they like for their fare. I have reached this conclusion after watching them for years. Every time I drove from my house to the gate one or two would fly up from a strip of grass down the middle of the road. I examined this grass, but could not see that it was different from the other wild species.

No need to ask, "Do I have the Indigo Bunting?" If you do have this beauty you will know it. It is like no other bird: blue all over, of an indescribable shade, different in different lights. "Indigo Bunting" is a stupid name; "Lapis Lazuli" would be more fitting. It is the size of an English Sparrow, but slimmer, and the little lady is almost the color of a Sparrow, which is a close relative.

"Here today and gone tomorrow" must be the motto of this much-desired creature. Some years they stayed with me all summer, building their nests in low twiggy shrubs, such as azaleas, but this time they left about the first of July. I did not find one nest. But if you want them leave some grass unmoved, for they must have the seeds!

The Painted Bunting is just as spectacular, showing an unbelievable combination of green, yellow, blue and red. To me he is not as beautiful as his cousin, the Indigo. But his gay coloring was his undoing, for before it became illegal many were trapped, caged and sold. In South Louisiana these bright birds are called "Pops" — a corruption of Pope. The Painted Bunting is not seen in hill country, but favors river courses. I have seen them only in willows along Cane River.

ROADRUNNER: GOOD CITIZEN

The first Roadrunner I ever saw, some years ago, was 'way over in Texas. He ran across the road in front of our old Ford, and was such an astonishing creature I could scarcely believe my eyes. Two feet long, he seemed to step a yard at each stride. He never did fly, just ran. It is said that his speed does not exceed fifteen miles per hour, but it *looks* faster. The tale is told that he can outrun a horse, but this is an exaggeration.

The August 1964 issue of "Arizona Highways" carried a delightful article, "The Roadrunner," by Willis Peterson. I was so enchanted with it I asked permission to quote some of the things he tells. Mr. Peterson has made an extended study of this fantastic bird and learned some little-known facts about him. He also relates legends that have grown up around this fascinating creature.

The Mexicans call him El Paisano — the Country-man — and love him. They encourage these birds to nest near their homes, for they are believed to bring good fortune. The Southwest Indians share this belief. Often mothers tie Paisano feathers to babies' cradles to protect the occupants from evil.

Because of his strange antics Roadrunner is referred to as "that crazy bird". But what could you expect? He belongs to the Cuckoo Family, so noted for queer behavior as to give rise to the slang expression, "You are just cuckoo!" One of the oddest things about this very odd bird is that two toes extend forward and two backward, so that one cannot tell from his tracks whether he is going or coming!

Some of the tallest tales relate the exploits of the Roadrunner in battling rattlesnakes. Now be it known the fellow isn't out just to exterminate these reptiles, he is simply getting food. With his lightning-swift movements he stuns the snake, then his powerful beak finishes him off. It is said that he scratches sand and dust in the snake's

92

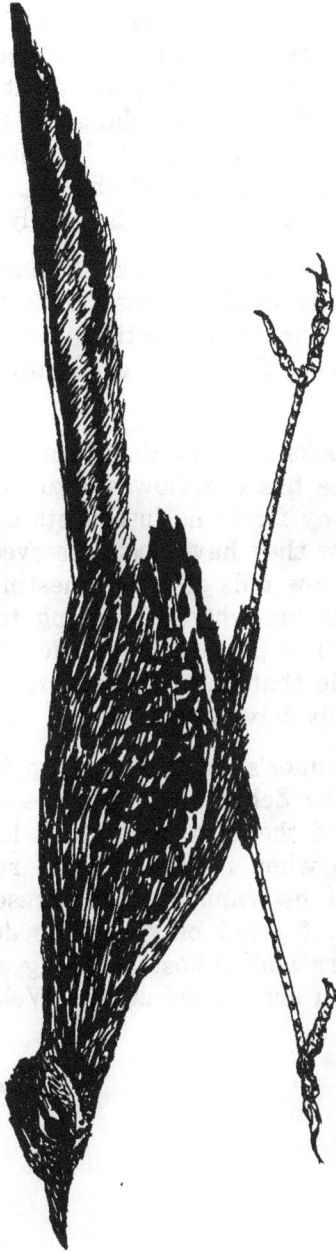

THE ROADRUNNER: "EL PAISANO"

eyes. After it is dead Paisano beats it to a hammered-steak consistency, then swallows it. If too long to be swallowed all at once Roadrunner goes about his business with the remainder of the snake dangling from his bill — which must be a comical sight! Of course his rapid digestive processes soon dispose of the appendage. If he finds the reptile too large to handle he wisely backs off.

His nest, in true Cuckoo fashion, is a loose pile of sticks, usually in a low bush. This friendly fellow likes to nest near human habitations and often builds in surprising places. The white eggs may number from three to seven.

The books give the Roadrunner as a bird of the Southwest, but he has overflowed into Louisiana. Several years ago I saw my first one in this state between my home and Castor. Now they have been observed in many localities. A farmer I know tells of a pair nesting quite near his home. The parents brought their young to his yard where they seemed fearless. Later, they made a second nest in a bunchy crape myrtle that had been cut off. I told this man that he should surely have good luck!

Roadrunner's camouflage is perfect. Just as the vivid stripes of the Zebra blend into the veldt, so do the streaks and spots of the bird blend with leaves and stems. He is easy to see when racing across a road, but when he runs into bushes he vanishes. His presence should surely be encouraged, for not only does he devour snakes, but also grasshoppers and almost anything else that runs or hops. Paisano, you are a good citizen. Welcome to Louisiana!

WAYFARERS OF THE SKY

The mind of man has always been intrigued by the migration of birds — that almost unbelievable movement of untold millions, of many species and all sizes, as if at a given signal. The question has always been "Why?" To this there is no satisfactory answer. Scientists offer the theory that a chemical change in their bodies tells them when to go. Perhaps this is true, but it does not tell them *where* to go!

Why do the Summer Tanager and Crested Flycatcher stop with us, while Scarlet Tanager and Rose-breasted Grosbeak merely pass through? In winter why do Fox Sparrows come back to the rocks where they fed last year, and in the spring the Wood Thrush shows up at the birdbath to drink and rest? This might be set down to memory. But why do Stormy Petrels go back to one tiny island in a vast ocean to nest? Instinct? It has been said that instinct is "inherited memory", so that must be what the Petrels possess.

"The Glacier Priest", who wrote a dramatic account of the stupendous eruption of Katmai in Alaska some years ago, tells a touching little story. He had visited the ancient crater when it was a lovely valley with a small stream and filled with trees and flowers. On his return after the tremendous explosion there were clouds of hot gases rising, but a pair of poor little White-throat Sparrows came back to build their nest. Utterly confused, they flew round and round till they fell into the hot crater. Why should White-throats leave an abundance of food and a mild climate to fly thousands of miles to their old breeding grounds? Why should tiny Kinglets make a similar journey to nest in the far North?

The only answer that would seem to answer all questions is that at some ancient time there were catastrophic changes in existing landmasses. Large islands disappeared and continents were greatly altered. Also, there were fantastic changes in climate. Lemmings swim off

95

into the sea and drown by thousands. Are they seeking a land that is no longer there?

We ground-dwellers have only the faintest conception of the concourse passing overhead during migration. Now and then a "bird shower" brings us a shock of realization. Once there was one at Winnfield and another at Arcadia. I did not see these, but those who did said the ground was covered with dead and dying birds "of all colors". Most of these were probably Finches and Warblers; Gold Finches, Indigo Buntings, Redstarts, etc. If they were flying high they could have passed into a stratum of extremely cold air in which they froze. Lighthouses blind migrants and thousands are destroyed. Once in Charleston there was a very low cloud-cover and masses of small birds pelted into

WHITE-THROATED SPARROW

This little wayfarer may travel from Louisiana to Alaska to rear his family.

lighted windows of dwellings. Dead and dying covered yards
and sidewalks.

The brave wild Geese start North before the cold is
over and sometimes have to turn back. The most amazing
little traveler of all is the Hummingbird. How can he store
up enough energy in that tiny body to carry him across the
Gulf of Mexico? It used to be thought that he stole rides on
the backs of large birds!

The birds' time-sense is almost perfect. Every year
at the same time in April — almost the same day — I hear
the sweet happy song of Orchard Oriole, the challenging
notes of Crested Flycatcher. Surely the White-throats
listen to the weather reports, for they never leave until
about the first day of May. They know that their destination
is a land of snow and ice until late spring.

Why does Chuck-Will's-Widow stay with us, while
his cousin, the Whip-poor-Will, goes right on farther
North? We may never know the answers to all these mys-
teries, but it is fascinating to go on asking and wondering.

WATER BRINGS BIRDS IN FREEZING WEATHER

During the severe freeze in December a lovely thing happened. It has always grieved me because Bluebirds would never come to feeding stations nor drinking vessels. On the coldest morning I was letting the water run at my kitchen sink — which empties right into the flowers — and the water was running fresh and clear. I looked down and there were four Bluebirds drinking. Entranced, I stood and watched. They kept coming and going, so I never did know how many there were. When I took a kettle of hot water and melted out the bird-bath, they came to that, too.

On the other side of the house, where I can watch from my bedroom window, I put cornbread crumbs in crevices in a low rock wall. Things were still frozen up the next morning, so I placed a hollowed-out rock there and filled it with water. In a short while there were four Bluebirds drinking at the same time — like a cluster of soft blue flowers. Of course I knew I had Bluebirds in my woods, for occasionally I heard their soft sweet warbles, but now I know how to bring them close when the weather gets rough. When pleasant days returned there were no more Bluebirds.

To my astonishment a flock of Cedar Waxwings came during this same freeze and drank from the hollow rock. These trim dandies had never done such a thing before, so I had two "firsts." With the cold, a flock of dainty Juncoes came and availed themselves of this convenient place to quench their thirst.

When everything is sheathed in ice Bluebirds die by the scores. Now I am convinced that one of the main causes is lack of water. It would seem that they require an unusual amount of this vital element.

Not only do birds drink a surprising amount of water in winter, but they also love to bathe — no mater how cold the weather. Wrens, Titmice and White-throats splash happily and sometimes just sit in the water, as if for pure pleasure. The big Brown Thrasher throws water about so prodigiously I wonder that any is left in the bird-bath!

Those who do not keep water available to the birds are being cruel to their friends and are depriving themselves of the opportunity for fascinating bird-watching.

BLUEBIRDS DRINKING FROM
HOLLOWED-OUT ROCK.

PLANT WINTER FOOD FOR BIRDS

This is going to be a hard winter for the birds. Because of late freezes last spring there are almost no berries. Here at Briarwood birds and squirrels have already stripped everything of fruit.

Every year the Robins devour the dogwood berries in front of my door, but when a flock came the other day they found not one. They sat around for a while in complete frustration and disgust, then departed. They probably went to the swamps to feed on Blackgum berries.

Lovers of wildlife should protest the wholesale deadening of hardwoods. Surrounding me vast tracts have been denuded of Beeches, Magnolias, Hickories, Blackgums, etc., and the starving squirrels are flocking to my place. In clearing woods for the growing of pines some discrimination could be used and foodtrees be spared.

Almost all home grounds contain plantings of Yaupon, Pyracantha, Viburnums and Magnolias, all of which supply food for birds during winter months. But other species can be added. Winter Huckleberry or Sparkleberry holds its fruit all winter and hungry little fellows flock to it when everything else fails. This is a big shrub or small tree that grows in hill country. It is quite ornamental, as the small leaves glisten as if shellacked and turn beautiful shades of red in winter, falling when it is almost spring. The small white flowers are borne in drooping racemes and look and smell like tiny Lilie-of-the-Valley. The shrubs are very twiggy and assume charming forms. Like all Huckleberries this one wants acid soil and good drainage.

Our beautiful Dogwood needs no description, but oddly enough many persons do not know of its beautiful red fruits. They are exceedingly bitter, but no one seems to mind. To my astonishment, I saw a Tufted Titmouse devouring them.

The numerous Viburnums — both native and exotic — offer winter food and are very ornamental. The Asiatic species usually have bright red berries, while most of the

BLACKHAW; Viburnum rufidulum

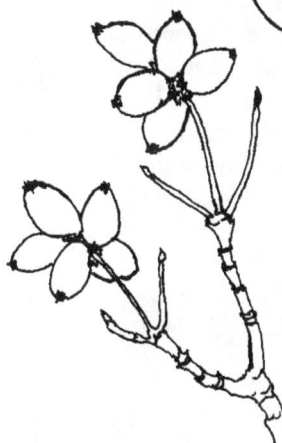

WINTER HUCKLEBERRY;
Vaccinium arboreum

DOGWOOD; Cornus florida

PLANT WINTER FOOD FOR BIRDS

natives bear clusters of blue fruits — some are first pinkish-rose, then black, quite attractive. Common old Blackhaw deserves more attention. A low spreading tree with shining leaves, it bears panicles of creamy flowers and in fall the clusters of berries, first rose then blue, are quite pretty. They cling until the little feathered ones devour them.

The dry-looking fruits of Sumac must contain some special food value, for I have even seen Bluebirds feasting on them when their natural food was sheathed in ice. Everyone knows the flaming fall foliage of the Sumac, but few seem to know that we have a species — Rhus glabra — which bears tight spikes of berries that are bright red till late winter.

We can plant these things for a future food supply, but while waiting for them to grow we must set the table for our birds now. The Finches, Cardinals, etc., are happy when given corn chops, but the insect-eaters must have more protein. Cornbread crumbs are best, but cracked nuts, suet, etc., are appreciated. After it gets hard, lumps of plain old tallow can be fastened in a wire container, hung in trees, and will delight the Woodpecker clan. Just don't forget to set the table for the birds!

WHEN THE LAST BIRDS SING

Listening to bird-song at dawn is a delightful experience. One by one the voices come in until there is a full chorus. I used to lie in bed and count as many as twenty different species identifying themselves by their characteristic notes. Now I can scarcely count six! What has happened?

Just two years ago James Stewart (Shreveport) said, "You have the heaviest population of Wood Thrushes that I have seen." Now there are *two!* Where have they gone? A few years ago, after a summer shower, the woods rang with their golden voices, seemingly a planned chorus.

Gone is the sprightly ringing song of the Louisiana Waterthrush — not a Thrush, really, but a Warbler. This shy little fellow haunted tiny streams, seldom seen, but always heard.

Dainty Wood Pewee used to sit on my light-wire by the hour, occasionally darting up to catch an insect on the wing, then returning to his perch. From a nearby tree I would hear the soft pleading note, "Plea-e-ease!" No more do I see or hear this little Flycatcher. Red-eyed Vireo used to "talk" incessantly all day long until it became monotonous. Now this valuable little bird is seldom heard.

Recently I read there was a reckless use of insecticides in some South American countries. On looking it up I found that most of these vanishing species winter in South America! This would seem to be the answer to the disappearance of many of our birds. Those that remain with me the entire year, such as Cardinal, Carolina Wren, Titmouse, etc., are as plentiful as ever.

But pointing an accusing finger at South America does not clear us of blame. Rachel Carson described the dreadful slaughter of bird life when D. D. T. was sprayed from the air to control Dutch Elm Disease. The U. S. Forest Service reported that the same practice, for the eradication of Spruce bud-worms, killed Chickadees, Nuthatches and

BROWN THRASHER
He scratches worms from the soil, and these may be
impregnated with D. D. T.

other small insectivorous species. The Service found another
pesticide to be used for this purpose.

In the fight for fire antcontrol the spreading of deadly
Heptachlor from planes destroyed so many birds and animals that a howl of protest was heard from all sides. Re-
sult, the Department of Agriculture found a substitute for
Heptachlor, which is said to be harmless. Research is in
progress to find harmless substitutes for the killers. This
should be strongly encouraged, for scientists have stated
that the present use of pesticides constitutes the greatest
threat to wildlife that has ever been known.

The public should demand that the spraying of D. D. T.
must go. It is one of the most deadly of insecticides, because it remains permanently in the body of all creatures.
Strange to say, it does not kill earthworms, but they become thoroughly impregnated with it. All Thrushes feed
on earthworms and thousands die annually. In mosquito
control campaigns D. D. T. is sprayed on mud around
pools. That fine game bird, the Woodcock, probes in mud
for worms, so many will be destroyed.

The advocates for the use of D. D. T. argue that it is
"cheap". Can anything be "cheap" that wipes out our
precious heritage of wildlife? A substitute can and must
be found for this lethal compound. Spraying poisons from
the air is a ghastly thing and scientists are discovering
other methods of control. The spectacular eradication of
the dreadful screwworm shows what could be done. But
these scientists are operating with utterly inadequate
funds. Congress should make a generous appropriation for
carrying on this vital work and curtail some of their
wasteful and destructive spraying programs.

The poor little birds have many natural enemies, Possums, Foxes, Armadilloes, but worst of all, snakes. And
this brings up the cat-snake controversy. Cat-haters cry,
"kill all the cats!" Many naturalists say "spare snakes, for
with the exception of a few poisonous species, they are
harmless." Hah! I have lived all my life with birds and I

state emphatically that more of our feathered friends are destroyed by snakes than by cats. All the Colubers can run up a tree, so no nest is safe from their depredations. One year my Brown Thrashers built three nests near the house and all were robbed by a big "Chicken-snake". Even the pretty little Grass-snake is not innocent — I caught one swallowing a Vireo's eggs.

In cities cats constitute more of a menace than snakes. Of course starving cats eat birds and should be disposed of. Sometimes the pampered pet is guilty too, but a cat can be taught not to catch birds if its owner begins when it is quite young. A kitten brings its first catch to receive praise. If it is a mouse praise should be given. If it is a bird, take it away, scold — a light slap may be necessary. Repeated a few times, this will convince any intelligent cat. My pet goes with me to feed the birds and never disturbs them. I have friends who scoff at this, but I tell them, "just try it."

But of all the animal kingdom Homo sapiens is the greatest threat to our beloved birds!

INDEX

INDEX

—A—

—B—

—M—

—N—

—O—

—P—

—Q—

—R—

—S—

—T—

—U—

—V—

—W—

—Y—

—Z—

www.ingramcontent.com/pod-product-compliance
Lightning Source LLC
Chambersburg PA
CBHW050215270326
41914CB00003BA/425